you & your
Mitsubishi
Shogun [Pajero/Montero]

you&your

Mitsubishi
Shogun [Pajero/Montero]

Paul Guinness *Buying, enjoying, maintaining, modifying*

Haynes

First published in August 2005

Paul Guinness has asserted his right to
be identified as the author of this work.

British Library cataloguing-in-publication data:
A catalogue record for this book is available
from the British Library

Published by Haynes Publishing,
Sparkford, Yeovil, Somerset BA22 7JJ, UK

Tel: 01963 442030 Fax: 01963 440001
Int. tel: +44 1963 442030 Int. fax: +44 1963 440001
E-mail: sales@haynes.co.uk
Website: www.haynes.co.uk

ISBN 1 84425 216 7

Library of Congress catalog card no. 2005925143

Haynes North America, Inc.,
861 Lawrence Drive, Newbury Park,
California 91320, USA

Printed and bound in Great Britain by
J. H. Haynes & Co. Ltd, Sparkford

Contents

Acknowledgements

I'd admired Mitsubishi's many Shogun and Pajero vehicles long before I started writing this book. Having driven most derivatives over the years, ever since the British launch of the original version in 1983, I'd always been impressed with their quality and their capabilities. Now, though, I'm also a big admirer of all the Shogun and Pajero owners out there.

The Shogun/Pajero has always enjoyed the very best customer loyalty of any 4x4. Once you've owned one, you'll invariably own another. And I'm grateful to all the enthusiastic owners who assisted me with this book, in particular for allowing me to photograph their vehicles.

Special thanks are also due to Frank Westworth, motoring editor, author and great friend, whose encouragement, humour and sheer enthusiasm at all times have been priceless.

I'm also particularly grateful to Rowena Hoseason (former Editor of *4x4 Mart*) for her support throughout these last few months, and to Emm Walters (current Editor of the same magazine) for her help, too. Thanks are also due to Richard Aucock for allowing me to use some of his own photographs in the book.

Finally, I'd like to mention Andy Carter, who has spent many years importing secondhand vehicles (and particularly Pajeros) from Japan, for allowing me to make the most of his vast experience. The lessons Andy has learned – often the hard way – have been particularly useful for this book.

I'm grateful to you all.

Paul Guinness
July 2005

Introduction

Since the early 1980s, Mitsubishi's amazingly successful Pajero has had a profound effect on the 4x4 scene, particularly throughout Europe. Who could have predicted way back in 1982 that Mitsubishi would take the all-wheel-drive market by storm and create a whole new class of 4x4 in the process?

The Pajero (also known as Shogun or Montero in certain markets, for reasons I'll come to later) wasn't Mitsubishi's first 4x4. That honour went to the Mitsubishi Jeep, a Japanese version of the all-American legend with its origins in World War II. But where the Mitsubishi Jeep was a crude and utilitarian affair, the all-new Pajero was a very sophisticated design.

The Pajero came to the market with the kind of sophistication and refinement previously reserved for buyers of the world-beating Range Rover. Yet, in typical Japanese style, it cost considerably less. No wonder it quickly established itself as a major player in the 4x4 market, and has continued to be so for almost a quarter of a century.

The Pajero and Shogun family has grown enormously over the years, yet all derivatives have retained the quality, capabilities and reliability associated with the brand. It's little wonder that, despite Mitsubishi's many financial woes of the early years of the 21st century, the Shogun/Pajero line-up has retained its loyal band of admirers around the globe.

The Pajero's success story continues – but why did Mitsubishi choose to use other model names for some of their export markets, a trend that continues today? In the UK, the Pajero has always been known as the Shogun – unless we're talking about an example unofficially imported from Japan, of course. Mitsubishi evidently thought British buyers would take more readily to the name of Shogun, particularly as a hugely successful TV series of the same name had been doing the rounds at about the time of the 4x4's launch.

In America and most Spanish-speaking markets, the Pajero has always been known as the Montero. It certainly sounds more American, a useful selling point in a country reared on such 'macho' 4x4 model names as Cherokee, Blazer, Explorer and the like. As for countries like Spain and the Canary Islands … well, Pajero wouldn't have been a suitable name at all. That's because Pajero is a slang word in Spanish referring to … how can I put this politely? … sexual self-

From its much-hyped debut in 1982, the Mitsubishi Pajero (and Shogun/Montero) has developed into one of the world's most highly respected 4x4 brands. *(Author)*

gratification. Not the ideal model name to use on an upmarket new 4x4.

The Pajero, Shogun and Montero story can get quite complicated at times, so I've done my best to keep things as simple as possible throughout the book, including my references to the different generations introduced over the years. That's why the 1982–1991 original-style Shogun/Pajero is referred to throughout as the Series I. Just as logically, I've referred to the newer-shape models of 1991–2000 as the Series II, despite some enthusiasts referring to later versions of these as the Series III; I feel they're far too similar in almost every way to demand a separate 'series' designation. Hence, my references to the Series III line-up are reserved for the all-new 2000-onwards models with their monocoque construction and curvaceous new styling.

It's not just the Pajeros and Shoguns themselves that

get complicated historically. There's also the lesser case of the original Mitsubishi Challenger being renamed the Pajero/Shogun/Montero Sport in most markets part-way through its life, as well as the arrival of the diminutive Pajero/Shogun Pinin range to expand the brand still further. Then there's the little matter of the Series I Pajero still being manufactured (at the time of writing) under licence in Korea, marketed as the Hyundai Galloper. Yes, it's a complex story, but one that I hope I've managed to unravel successfully.

Whatever your interest in Shoguns and Pajeros, this book will both entertain and inform. There's a full and detailed account of the history of this important 4x4 brand, as well as invaluable advice on buying, modifying and maintaining your Mitsubishi of choice. And if you want to know about 'grey' imports and all that the subject involves, you'll find an entire chapter dedicated to it.

No book quite like this, covering all the Pajeros, Shoguns and Monteros produced over the years, has been published before. It's been a long time coming, but I hope the wait has been worthwhile.

The square, boxy styling of the Series I family was perfect for its time. The long-wheelbase five-door model was a particularly useful version. *(Author)*

Above: The Series II offered a slightly softer, more modern look. Shown here is a fairly rare UK-spec convertible model. *(Author)*

Below: The reliability of the Shogun has given it plenty of appeal to the emergency services over the years. This Series III ambulance was a particularly effective conversion. *(Author)*

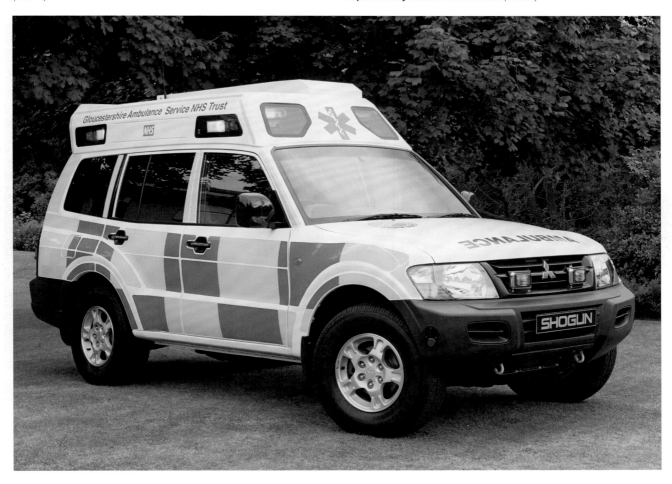

Chapter One

The early days

In today's headline-hungry world of the motoring media, it's easy for phrases such as 'trend-setting' or 'years ahead of its time' to be used and abused with scarcely a second thought when describing any new vehicle. And yet, in the case of the Mitsubishi Pajero – better known in the UK as the Shogun and in the USA and many Spanish-speaking countries as the Montero – it's hard to over-emphasise the importance of the model; or the effectiveness of its forward-thinking design; or, indeed, its enormous success throughout the world.

There are many onlookers who perhaps don't realise just what a vital contribution the Pajero and Shogun line-up has made to the all-wheel-drive scene since the early 1980s. Yes, they've seen the vehicles around, and probably even admired them from afar before dismissing them as '…just another big 4x4'. But to do this is to do Mitsubishi's most successful all-terrain vehicle a major disservice. In the same way that the Range Rover took Land Rover in a new, more upmarket direction at the start of the 1970s, so the Pajero and Shogun performed a similar feat for Mitsubishi a decade or so later.

Pre-Pajero times

Before the first Shoguns went on sale in the UK and most of mainland Europe (badged there as Pajero) in 1983, Mitsubishi wasn't a Japanese manufacturer we tended to associate with the world of 4x4s. That's because the kind of Mitsubishis most of Europe had seen on sale (since the end of 1974 in the case of the

UK) were worthy but straightforward saloons and hatchbacks, with the odd coupé or estate thrown in for good measure. Go looking for an all-wheel-drive, off-road Mitsubishi in the European line-up of the 1970s and you'd find the cupboard well and truly bare.

Interestingly – and rather bizarrely – the Mitsubishi name itself was kept in the background during the marque's early years on sale in Britain, the importer of the time preferring to use the Colt moniker instead. That meant such models as the Colt Lancer and Colt Sigma appearing, despite Colt being used as a single model name in later years.

This is how things looked pre-Pajero! An agreement with the Jeep Corporation saw this all-American icon being assembled in Japan and sold as a Mitsubishi. What it lacked in creature comforts it made up for in sheer robustness and durability. *(Mitsubishi)*

Don't underestimate the effect that different generations of Pajero, Shogun and Montero models have had on the world of 4x4s over the years. Shown here is a rather smart Series I long-wheelbase Pajero, a 'grey' import photographed in the UK. *(Author)*

THEY DON'T COME ANY TOUGHER THAN A MITSUBISHI JEEP.

When it comes to 4-wheel drive vehicles, one name is synonymous with rugged dependability. That name is Mitsubishi Jeep. Built to take the kind of punishment that difficult terrain and rough handling meet out, the Mitsubishi Jeep is a versatile, highly maneuverable, multi-purpose workhorse. Powerful traction gives it go-anywhere capability. A wide choice of models, features and options give it do-anything versatility. It works like a horse, drivers like a car, and offers maximum safety and comfort as well. Yet it is still smart enough to take into town. When the job calls for a 4-wheel drive vehicle, they don't come any tougher than a Mitsubishi Jeep.

It was the toughness of the Jeep that Mitsubishi were keen to exploit at the end of the 1970s. By this time it was a seriously aged product that, despite its many good points, was in dire need of replacement.
(Mitsubishi)

In 1984, Britain's Colt Car Company finally brought the Mitsubishi brand name to the forefront of its entire product line-up, with the Colt title being sidelined to an individual model rather than the marque as a whole. That's why, when the Shogun first went on sale in the UK in 1983, it was officially referred to as the Colt Shogun; by the following year, however, Mitsubishi Shogun had become its proper title – and that's how it would stay.

If Britain and the rest of Europe weren't used to Mitsubishi producing 4x4s prior to 1983, Japan certainly was. In fact, since the 1950s Mitsubishi had successfully produced its all-wheel-drive Jeep, badged as a Mitsubishi and built in Japan under licence from American Motors Corporation – then owner of the Jeep brand.

The Mitsubishi Jeep range was quite extensive, with soft-top and hard-top, short-wheelbase and long-wheelbase and petrol and diesel versions all available by the mid-1970s. Buyers also had a choice of four-, six-, seven- or nine-seater layouts, floor-shift or column-shift for the gearchange, plus various trim levels. But there was no disguising the sheer age of the Mitsubishi Jeep, an old design by any standards.

In fact, the Mitsubishi Jeep was very closely related to the Willys Jeep of World War II, the vehicle that had kept the Americans mobile throughout their involvement in the conflict, no matter how tough the terrain. The good old Willys was an almost indestructible off-roader that seemed to thrive on hard work and abuse. Ironically, post-World War II, it was also the vehicle that the Rover Car Company studied as its inspiration for the Series I Land Rover of 1948, thus helping to create what would become one of the world's most famous, most successful 4x4 marques of all time.

Talking of irony … how's this for a coincidence? Through the 1960s and '70s, the Jeep brand was owned by American Motors Corporation (AMC), which then licensed other companies worldwide to produce their own versions primarily for local consumption – including Mitsubishi. The 1980s saw Jeep being taken over by American giant Chrysler, which then merged with Germany's Daimler-Benz at the end of the 1990s, thus creating the DaimlerChrysler leviathan. In a bizarre twist of fate, DaimlerChrysler was one of Mitsubishi's largest shareholders, sharing production of the smart forfour and Mitsubishi Colt hatchbacks at the same Mitsubishi-owned factory in Holland.

There may no longer be a direct components-sharing relationship between the various off-road products of Mitsubishi and Jeep, but through several decades of company mergers, takeovers and collaboration, the close connection that once existed between the two marques – which created the tough and rugged Mitsubishi Jeep – still soldiers on, albeit in significantly different form. Few could have predicted 30 or more years ago that the Mitsubishi Jeep would have such historical significance.

From Jeep to Pajero

Successful as the Mitsubishi Jeep was, the end of the 1970s saw it facing new challenges and finding life difficult in an ever-evolving 4x4 market. Up until that point, the 4x4 scene was quite predictable, centred as it was around all-wheel-drive workhorses that offered few concessions to comfort or convenience. People bought 4x4s to do a specific tough-terrain job – a role in which the Mitsubishi Jeep genuinely excelled.

But times were changing. The success of the Range Rover throughout the 1970s showed that an all-conquering off-roader could also double up as family transport or even as an executive express. It was only a matter of time before this trend started filtering its way further downmarket, opening up all sorts of opportunities for 4x4 manufacturers willing to listen to the needs of a new breed of buyer.

6-seater Station Wagon			
J38R	Columnshift, RHD, Petrol engine 4G53	J36R	Columnshift, RHD, Diesel engine 4DR5
—		—	

6+250kg or 3+400kg

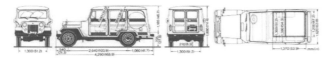

Above: The Jeep Six-Seater Station Wagon was arguably the closest thing to a Pajero that Mitsubishi had produced prior to the early 1980s. Despite its claims to be a family vehicle, it was still basic and utilitarian in style. *(Mitsubishi)*

Right: Mitsubishi's newcomer, marketed to most of the world as the Pajero, was known to the British as the Shogun. In the USA and many Spanish-speaking countries, Montero became the moniker of choice. It all seemed rather confusing at the time. *(Mitsubishi)*

With its Jeep range, though, there was only so much Mitsubishi could do. In the mid-1970s, the vehicle's ancestry already dated back more than three decades. And no matter how much Mitsubishi used such phrases as 'It works like a horse, drives like a car…', the Jeep was always going to be little more than a wartime leftover, with all that meant in terms of roughness and an alarming lack of creat**ure** comforts.

A market for the vehicle still existed, of course. Advertising copywriters claimed 'They don't come any tougher than a Mitsubishi Jeep', and they were right. Many buyers still praised it for its indestructible nature and its appetite for sheer hard work. But what Mitsubishi really needed was a new, more upmarket 4x4 that could take on the fresh challenges of the 1980s. Development work was soon under way.

A star is born

By the time the Mitsubishi Pajero was unveiled to the world's press in 1982, its existence was an open secret, but what perhaps shocked onlookers most was just what an amazingly competent machine it was. Anybody who suggested Mitsubishi knew nothing about producing 4x4s – apart from taking over an aged American design and producing it locally – would soon

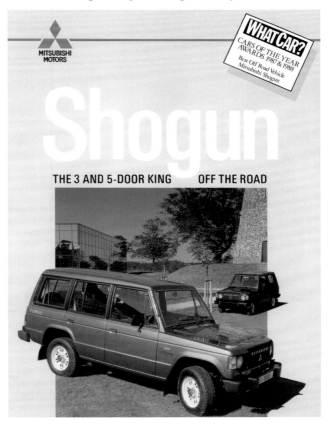

be eating their words. The all-new Mitsubishi Pajero was proclaimed a world-beater.

It wasn't that the Pajero was revolutionary in its design; far from it. It used a strong separate-chassis layout, just like a Range Rover. It offered a high level of passenger comfort and spaciousness, just like a Range Rover. It boasted impressive off-road capabilities, just like a Range Rover. And it came to most markets throughout the world at a price roughly half that of a Range Rover's. It was enough to send the management of Land Rover into a corporate panic attack.

In fairness to Mitsubishi, it never suggested the Shogun was a direct rival to the twice-the-price Range Rover, but the world's motoring press and, indeed, the buying public couldn't help drawing certain comparisons. And understandably so: after all, back in 1983, when this all-important newcomer from

With no direct rivals in sight, it wasn't long before the Shogun/Pajero was being compared with this – the legendary and hugely successful Range Rover. That the Mitsubishi was substantially cheaper to buy was the icing on the cake. *(BL Cars)*

Mitsubishi first went on sale in most export markets, nothing else quite like the Pajero existed.

This was a time when the 4x4 market was expanding rapidly but was still nowhere near as extensive as it is today. At the bottom of the price and size bracket sat the new Suzuki SJ line-up, tiny off-roaders costing roughly the same as most 'superminis'. Further up the sector were various Land Rover derivatives, later to be renamed Defender but still closely related to the agricultural-feeling workhorses that had made the brand so famous through the 1950s and '60s. And then there was the Range Rover, the 'off-road executive car' that cost more than just about any other 4x4 at the time.

In between, of course, Europe saw limited imports of models such as the Toyota Land Cruiser and Nissan Patrol – large, rugged off-roaders that fairly successfully bridged the gap between Land Rovers and Range Rovers. But back then, both these product lines placed more emphasis on off-road capabilities than on everyday usage – and their high list prices also scared off many potential buyers.

In 1983, therefore, most European markets were starved of what we now refer to as 'Discovery class' vehicles. That's because the launch of the Land Rover Discovery was still six years away; the Isuzu Trooper hadn't yet appeared; the Vauxhall/Opel Frontera (also to be developed by Isuzu) was barely a glint in its designer's eye; and the Nissan Terrano and Ford Maverick were still years away from conception, let alone actual arrival.

Almost overnight, the new Mitsubishi Pajero had succeeded in creating a whole new class of family 4x4 – but would buyers really take to the concept? The simple answer was 'yes'. But even the most optimistic expert couldn't have predicted the extent of the Pajero's influence throughout the 1980s and '90s.

The first Pajero to hit most markets in 1983 (including the UK, though it was badged as a Shogun) was the short-wheelbase model, a three-door version with angular, neat styling and a choice of petrol or diesel power. The petrol engine was a 2555cc four-cylinder unit producing a reasonably healthy 102bhp at 4500rpm, while fans of oil-burners were given a 2346cc four-cylinder turbo diesel with just 84bhp on tap, though this was increased to 2477cc capacity by 1987 – with no initial increase in power output but with 11 per cent extra bottom-end torque for added off-road and towing capabilities. These engines represented a good

The first Pajero on sale in Europe in 1983 was the three-door short-wheelbase model, available with a choice of 2.6-litre petrol or 2.3-litre diesel power. Sales boomed almost overnight – it was the 4x4 that buyers had been waiting for. *(Richard Aucock)*

enough choice for the Pajero/Shogun's introduction, satisfying two very distinct buyer groups along the way.

In the UK in particular, the three-door Shogun was marketed as an all-terrain fun vehicle (particularly in petrol guise), aimed at the kind of folk who didn't need five-door versatility or seven-seater spaciousness. It wasn't agricultural, but it would prove to be a decent off-roader. It wasn't luxurious, but it was comfortable and well equipped. It wasn't a Range Rover … but, at half the price, did anyone really care?

It was inevitable that Mitsubishi would be keen to expand the Pajero/Shogun line-up still further, which is why October 1984 saw the British launch of the five-

Half the price of a Range Rover in the UK, the new three-door Shogun was soon selling well beyond expectations. Shown here is a 2.5 TD from 1989, sold at auction in 2004 for a very reasonable £1450. *(Author)*

door long-wheelbase models. This is when the Shogun really grew up, for the five-door derivatives were aimed at a very different buyer group. These were big vehicles

by any standards, and were the perfect buy for anybody seeking a spacious, competent, family-style off-roader. These were the versions whose success would directly lead to the creation by Land Rover of the Discovery five years later. These were the Shoguns that frightened the competition the most.

Under the skin

Apart from their obvious difference in size and the number of doors, the short- and long-wheelbase Pajeros/Shoguns shared the same basic layout. Each boasted a sturdy but conventional ladder-frame steel chassis, a principle shared with every other 4x4 of the early 1980s. Where the Pajero/Shogun differed, though, was in its use of independent front suspension, a set-up that comprised twin wishbones and torsion bars. The result of this was a ride quality better than that of any other 4x4 this side of a Range Rover, plus a level of on-road handling that put Solihull's rather 'roly-poly' top product in the shade.

It was a remarkable achievement, quite unexpected in this new market segment. All-wheel-drive vehicles

An early publicity shot for the new five-door Shogun shows how much more 'grown up' the latest version seemed. It would appeal to a very different kind of buyer than the three-door, proving to be a family 4x4 in a class of its own. *(Mitsubishi)*

the size of the short-wheelbase Pajero had traditionally been harsh, bouncy and relentlessly uncomfortable; but this newcomer from Mitsubishi was different. And in five-door form, the ride was improved still further – not unexpectedly, given the longer wheelbase of that version.

The impressive specification didn't end there. Unlike the more up-market Range Rover, the Pajero and Shogun used a part-time four-wheel-drive set-up, relying on rear drive for normal on-road use only. This meant a reduction in driveline drag, which in turn meant improved potential fuel economy figures. The Range Rover might have boasted better ultimate grip on wet or greasy roads thanks to its permanent four-wheel drive, but it has always been a simple task to select four-wheel drive on any Pajero or Shogun.

That's thanks to Mitsubishi's dual-range transfer box. It was a chain-driven design, which meant uncommonly low transmission noise levels, another boost to the Pajero's refinement claims. With one simple move of the transfer box lever, a Pajero could be instantly transformed from rear-wheel drive to high-ratio four-

wheel drive – ideal for mild off-roading or for on-road use during particularly bad weather conditions. For more serious off-roading, of course, it was just as easy to then select low-ratio all-wheel drive, a setting that proved particularly successful in the diesel-engined versions of those early Pajeros and Shoguns.

Low-ratio four-wheel drive is what serious off-roaders tend to rely on in extreme conditions. Combine the effectiveness of the Mitsubishi's system with the high torque levels and impressive low-down pulling power of the Shogun/Pajero's 2.5-litre turbo-diesel engine and you've got a competent mix. The oil-burner's 84bhp might not have been outstanding for an engine of this capacity, but a torque figure of 148lb ft at a commendably low 2000rpm was extremely useful, comparing favourably with the petrol version's 142lb ft at 2500rpm. The difference might not seem that great,

What the turbo-diesel Shogun lacked in outright power, it made up for in decent torque levels – a major aid when off-roading. Part-time four-wheel drive and a dual-range transfer box were part of the fixtures and fittings. *(Mitsubishi)*

but the diesel engine's low-revving character and its seemingly unstoppable ability to power its way at tickover speed through even the toughest challenges stood it in good stead in this instance.

Incidentally, whenever a Shogun was switched to either of its all-wheel-drive settings, the free-wheel

WHAT THE PRESS SAID:
Series I Shogun/Pajero

Despite the claimed 8.3in ground clearance, it gets bogged down as soon as it looks at soft sand or deep mud. On paper the Pajero has more ground clearance than a Range Rover, but it has much more underneath to catch, and poor rear overhang on the long wheelbase. It is soon bogged down if it tries to follow the ruts made by Land Rovers or Range Rovers, often being shown up by the little Lada Nivas and Suzukis.

The Off-Road Four Wheel Drive Book by Jack Jackson (1988 edition)

front hubs fitted as standard came into practice, automatically disengaging themselves when rear drive was selected once again. It was another useful feature that helped to ensure this tough new Mitsubishi was a capable off-road machine – maybe not to traditional Land Rover standards, but remarkable for a vehicle offering such impressive refinement.

Indeed, whether buyers chose a petrol- or a diesel-engined Shogun, they often found themselves impressed with the refinement of the powerplant itself. This was thanks to Mitsubishi's unique Silent Shaft system of the time, which consisted of two counter-rotating balancer shafts operating at twice the engine speed. The lower one was above the top of the crankshaft, rotating in the opposite direction to the crank, while the upper one was halfway up the engine block and rotated in the same direction as the crank. The load of each was supported by a bulkhead in the middle of the block, and the end result was a dramatic reduction in engine vibration and a noticeable improvement in refinement.

So effective was this Silent Shaft technology that Mitsubishi subsequently licensed it to Porsche for use in the 944 sports car – but that's another story. All we need to know here is that the all-new Shogun/Pajero was one of the most civilised and easy-to-live-with off-roaders the world had ever seen. And that alone was enough to win it many friends.

The going's good

Mitsubishi never intended its Shogun (or Pajero) to be a performance machine – which is a good job, particularly in the case of the turbo-diesel version. In five-door long-wheelbase guise in particular, the diesel-powered Shogun was a lethargic beast out on the road. According to Britain's *Autocar* magazine, which tested a Shogun 2.5 TD five-door back in May 1987, the vehicle was capable of just 83mph, and would take a yawning 17.8 seconds to reach 60mph from standstill. Even by diesel standards of the time, those weren't impressive figures; but to castigate the Shogun for being sloth-like would be to miss the point entirely.

You see, no 'ordinary' Shogun or Pajero was ever about speed or performance. It was more about useable power, adequate torque and, above all else, reliability and dependability – two factors that Mitsubishi had become renowned for over the years. Why else would this innovative Japanese manufacturer become the first to offer a three-year unlimited-mileage warranty on all its models sold throughout Europe? Few rivals dared to match this high level of confidence back in the 1980s.

Even so, there was a proportion of Shogun and Pajero buyers for whom a mere 84bhp wasn't enough – which is why the four-cylinder OHC petrol-engined version proved immediately popular, particularly in the UK where sales of diesel cars were still very much in the minority in the mid-1980s. With 102bhp of useful power on tap, the petrol Shogun's top speed was a more

Petrol or diesel power, the Shogun/Pajero offered all the advantages of Mitsubishi's Silent Shaft technology – quite an innovation back in the early 1980s. Shown here is a 2.5-litre diesel unit. *(Author)*

To criticise any early Shogun/Pajero five-door for its lack of outright speed or acceleration would be to miss the point entirely. More importantly, the newcomer was strong, durable, reliable and never afraid of hard work. *(Author)*

respectable 88mph, with the 0–60mph 'dash' in a healthier 14.5 seconds (or thereabouts, depending on whether you were driving a short- or a long-wheelbase version). It was also a more refined drive, lacking the traditional diesel 'clatter' and higher noise levels of the oil-burning versions. But, naturally, there was a price to pay at the fuel pumps.

Using the official UK fuel consumption figures of the 1980s as a guide proves the point. On the urban cycle, a 2.6-litre petrol-engined Shogun five-door would return a claimed 17.1mpg, compared with a far healthier 27mpg for the turbo-diesel equivalent. At a steady 75mph, the difference was almost as dramatic – 20mpg versus just 17.5mpg; and at a constant 56mph (the most economical part of the official test cycle in the 1980s), the numbers were 25.9mpg for the petrol and

It didn't take long for the three- and five-door Shoguns and Pajeros to appeal to a wide range of buyer types, the short-wheelbase derivatives being the most affordable models on offer.

(Richard Aucock)

31mpg for the diesel. Such figures couldn't always be replicated in everyday use, but there was no denying that a petrol-powered Shogun would always be significantly less economical than its diesel cousin – and for anybody paying their own fuel bills, that was a major consideration.

No wonder that when a V6-engined version of the first-generation Shogun/Pajero appeared in many key markets, it was destined to be seen as very much a niche model. With a 2972cc V6 pumping out 141bhp and 166lb ft of torque, this five-door-only version was a mighty machine by any standards – and was arguably the closest that the early Shogun would ever get to being a true Range Rover rival. But with fuel economy averaging the low to mid-teens in everyday use, the Shogun/Pajero V6 was never going to appeal to large numbers of buyers. Still, it provided Mitsubishi with a useful flagship model, and helped to lift the Shogun's image still further. It didn't take long for the Shogun and Pajero to be seen as highly desirable among certain sectors of the car-buying public.

The class system

That Mitsubishi managed to come up with such a fantastically competent 4x4 at virtually the first attempt said a lot about the skills of the company's designers and engineers. That the European (and in particular the British) public took to the newcomer in such an overwhelming manner said even more about the company's ability to reinvent its own image virtually overnight.

So who exactly was buying the new Shogun? Pretty much anybody who could afford one at the time, for these weren't cheap vehicles – despite their ability to make a Range Rover look hugely overpriced. By 1988, for example – roughly halfway through the Shogun's life – the least expensive version on offer in Britain was the petrol-engined 2.6 three-door at £12,289. Those with deeper pockets could 'invest' up to £17,215 in a Shogun 2.5TD five-door with Diamond Option Pack (which we'll come to later) at the other extreme of the range. These were fairly hefty sums by the standards of the late 1980s. But that didn't deter buyers from almost literally queuing up to buy their Shoguns; in fact, by 1988, the Shogun accounted for a massive 22 per cent of all sales in the expanding off-road sector of the UK market.

The Shogun quickly established itself as a popular buy with people who towed caravans, horseboxes, boats and trailers. In Britain, Mitsubishi started sponsoring the Badminton Horse Trials, thus promoting its image still further in front of an audience with – in general – higher than average disposable incomes; and within a couple of years, Shoguns were a common sight on caravan sites, at horse events and parked near boat slipways throughout the UK. Never before had there been a 4x4 on sale that doubled up as family transport and first-class towing vehicle in quite the same way.

Particularly useful were the Shogun's maximum towing weights, which started off healthy but were dramatically increased in 1987. To begin with, all Shoguns offered a maximum braked towing capacity of 3969lb. By 1987, this had increased to 6173lb for the three-door and a massive 7275lb for the five-door. Those who needed one of the ultimate towing vehicles available at any price suddenly had very little excuse for not buying a Shogun/Pajero.

The three- and five-door Shoguns, given their varying levels of versatility and accommodation, appealed to quite different buyers. The three-door was strictly a four- or five-seater, with a reasonable amount of luggage space behind the folding rear seat; it was aimed at a younger buyer than the long-wheelbase models, and appealed to those who didn't have large families to consider.

The five-door, by comparison, was a far more adaptable machine. Thanks to three forward-facing rows of seats, it offered accommodation for up to seven people, though boot space was obviously severely limited when so many were on board. Yet fold the two rearmost seats away and you had a genuine five-seater vehicle with a massive amount of room for luggage and other paraphernalia. Or you could fold the centre seat flat and have a two-seater all-terrain vehicle with the

With three rows of forward-facing accommodation, the five-door Shogun/Pajero was a genuine seven-seater. The rearmost seats folded up into the sides of the luggage area when not in use. (Mitsubishi)

carrying capacity of a reasonably sized van. This was versatility in the extreme, and quite a breakthrough by the standards of the early 1980s.

Automatically better

Further proof of the Shogun's reputation as a civilised machine was its availability in automatic guise – albeit only as a five-door turbo diesel for several years. This in itself was an unusual move, as most car markets weren't used to diesel-powered automatics in the mid-1980s. But Mitsubishi was convinced there would be demand for such a machine, a hunch that proved to be true.

Not as many European Shogun/Pajero buyers chose the automatic option as did the Japanese. In Mitsubishi's homeland, the Pajero of choice has always been a turbo-diesel linked to auto transmission, no doubt a response to that country's generally overcrowded streets. Even so, increasing numbers of early British Shogun buyers found

WHAT THE PRESS SAID:
Shogun TD 5-Door

With its new engine, the smooth-performing Shogun turbo-diesel is the best Land Rover alternative. The interior offers masses of accommodation but lacks the class of the Discovery's. Equipment levels are high, but then so is the price. In LWB form it's £2500 more than our (Discovery 200 TDi) winner.

What Car? magazine's Car Of The Year – April 1990

Although not as popular in Europe as in Japan, the Shogun/Pajero's option of automatic transmission managed to expand the model's appeal still further. Few other diesel-engined autos were available in the Eighties. *(Mitsubishi)*

themselves tempted by the four-speed automatic transmission that was on offer.

Essentially of three-speed-plus-overdrive design, it was a smooth and effective gearbox that proved refined and low-revving at motorway speeds and an absolute boon on urban roads. Even for off-roading, the set-up

Where the sun tended to shine more than in the UK, the Shogun/Pajero Convertible was a popular choice. Shown here is a Spanish-spec Montero, photographed in 2004 in the Canary Islands. *(Author)*

in a Shogun Automatic proved competent thanks to the facility to lock the transmission in second or third gear – a useful feature when using the engine's low-down torque to power its way through the toughest terrain.

Nowadays, first-generation turbo-diesel Shoguns with auto transmission are relatively unusual in Britain, given the age of the vehicles. However, a very large proportion of the imported early Pajeros can still be found with this specification. So if the idea of an early turbo diesel with an auto 'box appeals, you'll probably find yourself at the wheel of a Pajero rather than a Shogun – although, as we'll discover further on in the book, that's no bad thing.

Changes and updates

It's easy to glance at any first-generation Shogun or Pajero and assume the model changed hardly at all during its eight years in production. However, a number of important but often subtle updates did occur over time, not least on British-spec Shoguns; imported Pajeros will be dealt with in far greater depth in Chapter Five.

At this point we should certainly mention the convertible version of the short-wheelbase Shogun – a rarity in the UK but a model that, in Pajero and Montero guises, went on to prove popular in warmer climes. It was an attractive-looking machine, with a well-made hood that – usually finished in black – seemed to suit the squareness of the Shogun's styling rather well. It wasn't the easiest hood in the world to lower and raise in a hurry, but it was a decent-quality item.

The Series I Shogun Convertible's short period on sale in Britain probably wasn't just down to the UK's unpredictable weather and high rainfall levels. I'd suggest most British 4x4 buyers of the early 1980s probably weren't ready for an unashamed 'leisure' version of the Shogun; it was simply the wrong vehicle at the wrong time. Within a few years, though, the market for convertible 4x4s would be expanding rapidly (look to the Suzuki Samurai and Vitara Soft-Top for proof), so it's a shame Mitsubishi's British operations missed out for a while.

It was better news elsewhere for the Pajero and Montero Convertibles, however, and it's not unusual to see rag-top versions of each when you're holidaying somewhere warm. In mainland Spain and the Canary

With the hood removed from over the rear seats, this Montero Convertible makes a great summer fun car. Two sideways-facing rearmost seats turn this into a rather unlikely seven-seater, though! *(Author)*

Islands, in particular, soft-top Monteros aren't a rare sight – and can occasionally still be seen as (now rather elderly) hire cars. Their hoods tend to be 'down' or 'off' for months on end, which makes these Mitsubishis terrific fun to drive in such a climate.

Moving on to the five-door versions of the Series I Shogun/Pajero, one of the most noticeable differences between various models was their roof height, as this varied depending on the age and specification of the individual vehicles. Early five-door Shoguns tended to have what we now refer to as the high roofline, though a lower roofline became available shortly after launch. By 1987 though, the high roofline was phased out

The high roofline, standard on the very earliest five-doors, became an option soon after launch, before being phased out altogether in 1987. Seen here is a Spanish-spec Montero with its original high roof. Not ideal for multi-storey car parks... *(Author)*

altogether, mainly because of difficulties Shogun owners were experiencing when tackling multi-storey car parks or trying to get into a normal car-sized garage. The lower roofline certainly made the longer Shogun a much more practical vehicle for day-to-day use.

This wasn't the only change during 1987, as this was the year when the Shogun received a couple of important mid-life updates. Most significant was the announcement of Mitsubishi's new three-year, unlimited-mileage warranty and six-year anti-corrosion guarantee – both unmatched (as a combination) by any rival of the time. It was also the year when, as mentioned earlier in this chapter, the cubic capacity of the turbo-diesel engine was slightly increased, creating extra torque in the process.

The following year, 1988, saw more (albeit relatively minor) changes. The Shogun's instrument panel was updated, a new design of steering wheel was adopted, some extra paintwork colours were introduced, an anti-slam mechanism was announced for the tailgate and the rear wash/wipe unit was given a useful intermittent setting. None of these changes set the world alight, but they were worthwhile. In any case, with sales of the Shogun/Pajero still booming worldwide, what was the need for anything more complicated?

By now, Mitsubishi's extra-cost 'Diamond Option Pack' was also proving a popular choice with five-door Shogun buyers, endowing the vehicle with a limited-slip differential and electric windows all round.

Incidentally, at this stage (for reasons best known only to Mitsubishi) the Shogun Automatic was the only version to come with central door-locking as standard – a strange quirk of early Shogun specifications.

The end was nigh

Nothing lasts forever, and the first-generation Shogun was no exception. A defining moment came in 1989, when Land Rover launched its vital new Discovery model, the toughest competition the Shogun/Pajero would ever face. With more modern, more distinctive styling than the Shogun, the Discovery had a great deal going for it; Mitsubishi couldn't sit back and do nothing indefinitely.

It wasn't just the Discovery that started giving the original Shogun a harder time towards the end of its life. The Isuzu Trooper had arrived on the British scene by 1987 and was quickly establishing itself in the 4x4 market. It might not have been as refined or as upmarket as most Shoguns, but the Trooper offered great value and was a formidable off-road machine.

It's a tribute to Mitsubishi that such rivals appeared at all. It proved that the market for Shogun-type vehicles, which Mitsubishi had effectively created single-handedly, still had enormous potential worldwide. But that meant new, tough competition for the Shogun and Pajero.

When the second-generation Shogun finally went on sale in 1991, it wasn't a moment too soon. But would

How's this for snazzy 1980s gear and a Shogun overloaded with aftermarket goodies? Mitsubishi's various Diamond Options became popular with buyers looking for a bit more individuality. *(Mitsubishi)*

Mitsubishi fans take to the newcomer with the same enthusiasm that had greeted the original model – and was the latest version improved enough to provide the higher standards expected in the 1990s?

By the end of the 1980s, the Series I Shogun/Pajero was starting to look rather dated; its boxy, square styling was now in need of freshening up. Reliability alone could no longer guarantee major sales success. *(Author)*

Chapter Two

Next generation

Eight years of European success, complemented by a major following in both Japan and the United States, had made the original-style Shogun/Pajero quite a money-spinner for Mitsubishi. In fact, it had evolved into one of the company's best-selling export products, but the start of the 1990s saw it facing numerous fresh challenges.

The launch of the Land Rover Discovery mentioned in Chapter One was bad news for the Shogun. Indeed, the Solihull product had had almost two years of sales success under its wheels before the second-generation

Shogun hit the streets, enabling the Discovery to go straight to the top of the 4x4 sales charts in the UK and many other European countries. The Shogun suddenly found itself in the unenviable position of playing catch-up, which meant a tough start in life for the Series II line-up.

Yet Mitsubishi needn't have worried. Whilst the British-built Discovery had made the original-shape Shogun look alarmingly dated, the UK announcement of a new line-up of restyled models in April 1991 soon brought attention back to the Mitsubishi marque. And, crucially, the new-generation Shogun/Pajero range would – as with its predecessor – be available with a choice of two wheelbases, a major advantage over the Discovery.

The arrival of the Series II Shogun/Pajero line-up in 1991 – two years after the Land Rover Discovery – saw Mitsubishi back at the top of the 4x4 tree. The restyling exercise was a major success.

(Mitsubishi)

Smooth new looks

Trying to make a 4x4 off-roader look smooth, sleek and sexy is a difficult task at the best of times, but in that respect, the second-generation Shogun/Pajero couldn't really have failed. The Series I models, after all, had been as boxy, upright and unadventurous in their styling as it was possible to be; yes, they looked good, but they could never be described as 'over-styled'.

No wonder the second-generation line-up of 1991 appeared to be so different. Where the original Shogun looked as if it had been drawn with the aid of a ruler, the latest versions employed radical shapes such as curves. It had soft edges, stylised bumpers and a whole lot more. At last, here was a 4x4 that felt as though somebody had put a lot of thought into how it looked, not just how it performed.

It was an important change of approach for Mitsubishi, given that the newcomers were about to take the Shogun/Pajero brand further upmarket than it had ever dared go in the 1980s. The 3.0-litre V6 model – introduced during the final years of the Series I's career – continued with the second-generation models, but came better equipped and smoother riding than ever before. It was now a genuine alternative to the likes of the Range Rover or top-of-the-range Discoverys. The Shogun had grown up; and how.

As with the launch of the Series I models, it wasn't just the choice of short or long wheelbases that dictated the Shogun/Pajero's options style-wise: it wasn't long before a convertible version of the Series II was on sale, offering a similar kind of two-piece soft-top arrangement as the Series I rag-top, along with a roll-up plastic rear window and removable rear sides. The end result looked good and, as with its predecessor, attracted a great deal of interest in countries with favourable weather; in the UK, once again, the Convertible's success was limited.

But why? So much had changed since the launch of

The Shogun/Pajero V6 was continued in Series II guise, initially with the same-capacity 3.0-litre engine. The top of the range Discovery and the mighty Range Rover were now well and truly within Mitsubishi's sights. *(Mitsubishi)*

Fans of the Convertible weren't forgotten when the Series II went on sale, hence the arrival of this latest version. Shown here is a German-registered Pajero Convertible – less than pristine but still very much in use. *(Author)*

The Series II's 4x4 set-up was improved by the new 'shift-on-the-fly' facility, allowing high-ratio four-wheel drive to be selected at speeds of up to 62mph. It was a useful innovation, aiding the Shogun/Pajero's growing reputation as an off-road machine.
(Mitsubishi)

the Series I Convertible, after all. Suzuki's 4x4 soft-tops were proving more popular than their hard-top derivatives by now, so it wasn't as if British buyers were still unused to the idea of a canvas-roofed 4x4. Perhaps it was more to do with the fact that the latest Shogun range was more upmarket than before, and buyers spending substantial sums of money on what many saw as a Range Rover rival simply weren't the kind of folk to choose a convertible 4x4. The little Suzukis, after all, were basic, tiny, crude and aimed unashamedly at the 'fun' market. But the seriously more grown-up Shogun was a different kind of vehicle entirely, and British buyers weren't prepared to buy the Convertible in sufficient numbers to prevent it from experiencing a rather short lifespan.

It wasn't just the Shogun/Pajero's styling that had been upgraded with the Series II, of course, but the whole technical specification, too. The chassis was still a traditional ladder-frame design, giving it strength and

rigidity, particularly when off-roading; but standard technical equipment now included rear disc brakes instead of drums, coil-sprung suspension, an intercooler on turbo-diesel versions and a brand new four-wheel-drive set-up going by the name of Super Select. Meanwhile, buyers who paid extra for the new Shogun's Diamond Pack option would also be treated to ABS brakes, variable-rate suspension and even an electronic compass.

On all fours

The latest Shogun's all-wheel-drive system was, from a technical point of view, still influenced by the previous design, retaining the concept of a part-time dual-range transfer box. The big difference now was that high-ratio four-wheel drive could be selected at speeds of up to 100km/h (62mph). It was a far more adaptable system and vastly more practical.

It meant that on-road occurrences demanding all-wheel traction could now be dealt with instantly, without having to bring the vehicle to a standstill in order to switch from rear-wheel drive to all-wheel drive. In countries such as the UK, with its varied climate and unpredictable winter weather, it proved particularly popular.

Various products from Land Rover may have offered superior axle articulation when the going got tough, but the Mitsubishi's locking diff and dual-range all-wheel drive were proving more than adequate for most buyers. *(Mitsubishi)*

This kind of system is commonly referred to as 'shift-on-the-fly' (an American term), and it's now considered the norm for 4x4s built since the mid-1990s. In 1991, though, Mitsubishi was the first company to use it in the 'affordable family 4x4' market, and it helped the latest-generation Shogun/Pajero to grab yet more headlines the world over.

This latest innovation made little or no difference to off-road capabilities. Mild off-roading would require high-ratio all-wheel drive from the start anyway, while the selection of low-ratio four-wheel drive when the going got extra tough still involved bringing the vehicle to a standstill before moving the transfer box lever that extra notch.

As an off-road machine, the second-generation Shogun/Pajero was very much in the same league as its predecessor. There were – and still are – more competent off-roaders around (the Land Rover Defender, to name just one), but none of them offered the same kind of on-road refinement and driver-friendliness that the Mitsubishi boasted.

But the latest Shogun did have one more trick up its sleeve. With low-ratio all-wheel drive selected, the driver was able to lock the rear differential, which gave a welcome and very useful extra boost to overall

traction. Combine the locking diff and all-wheel grip with the low-down torque of the 2.5-litre turbo-diesel engine and you had the perfect recipe for seriously accomplished off-roading.

Unfortunately, the Shogun/Pajero's relative lack of front-wheel articulation would always allow the Land Rover an edge in truly inhospitable terrain. But with everything else in its favour, the latest 4x4 from Mitsubishi offered far more off-road capability than most owners would ever need.

As before – and for obvious reasons – it was the short-wheelbase Shogun/Pajero that proved the most competent in the rough. When variable-rate suspension was specified (arguably a bit of a gimmick, but still an interesting offering), it was possible to make just the right selection for your particular off-road needs.

Yet, despite its promise of improved rough-stuff abilities, the Series II Shogun/Pajero found most of its off-road work restricted to caravan sites, beaches and yacht clubs, so accomplished was the newcomer as a top-class towing vehicle. Indeed, it didn't take Britain's Caravan Club very long to realise the latest Shogun's prowess as a tow car, and in 1995, *Practical Caravan* magazine awarded the Shogun turbo diesel five-door

The Series II models were some of the most highly praised of the time when it came to their capabilities as tow cars. The Shogun/Pajero has received numerous towing awards throughout its career, the Series II probably claiming the most success. *(Mitsubishi)*

the accolade of Best Off-Roader in its Readers' Top Towing Car competition. The Discovery may have taken a huge chunk of the family-size 4x4 market since 1989, but the Shogun was to retain its reputation as one of the finest towing vehicles in the world throughout the 1990s.

Power source

When the second-generation Shogun/Pajero was unveiled, what lay beneath the bonnet was all very familiar stuff to most onlookers. The old 2.6-litre four-cylinder engine had been discontinued, though, leaving just the 2972cc V6 powerplant (introduced towards the end of the Series I's life) to keep fans of petrol power happy. Now pumping out 147bhp at 5000rpm (a boost of 6bhp over the previous version), it was a powerful, impressively smooth and very desirable engine choice for buyers of long-wheelbase Shoguns – as long as they could afford to pay for its prohibitively high fuel consumption.

Far more practical was the good old 2477cc four-cylinder turbo diesel, now fitted with an intercooler as

standard. With other minor mods to add to its appeal, this engine suddenly had a far more useful 105bhp (at 4200rpm) at its disposal instead of the miserly 84bhp offered in its original incarnation. Even more important was the diesel's increase in torque, rising from a respectable 148lb ft to a significantly more useful 177lb ft at just 2000rpm.

On the road, these improved figures translated into a top speed of 91mph, a useful 8mph increase over the previous 2.5-litre diesel, and while standing-start acceleration didn't feel vastly quicker, the engine's extra flexibility, low-down torque and increased power meant fewer gear changes and an altogether more relaxing driving experience. It was still no ball of fire, but at least a diesel-powered Shogun could now keep up with traffic flow with far less effort.

Mitsubishi didn't leave the engine range alone for very long, though. As the 1990s progressed, so more 4x4 rivals started to appear – and, once again, Mitsubishi needed to stay one step ahead of the competition, which is why, from 1994, long-wheelbase diesel-powered Shoguns were given a boost in the

shape of a 2835cc version of the four-cylinder turbo diesel, this time pumping out an impressive 123bhp at 4000rpm, with torque massively boosted to 215lb ft at 2000rpm. At last, a five-door diesel-powered Shogun could be ordered with the kind of power and performance levels it had always deserved, making it more than a match for all the turbo-diesel Discoverys and Troopers that were now proving so popular.

Perhaps understandably, Mitsubishi chose to retain 2.5-litre propulsion for the turbo-diesel Shogun three-door throughout the life of the Series II range, as this was thought to be adequately powerful for a relatively compact 4x4; and they may well have been right. It's just a shame it took them until 1994 – a full decade since the launch of the original five-door Shogun – to get around to seriously boosting the power of the larger version.

The smallest petrol engine available in a Series II Shogun/Pajero was the 3.0-litre V6 – further proof of Mitsubishi's determination to push its hugely successful 4x4 even further upmarket. Seen here is a Spanish-registered V6 three-door. *(Author)*

It took Mitsubishi until 1994 to enlarge their turbo-diesel Shogun/Pajero powerplant. The eventual arrival of the 2.8 TD meant extra power and torque, as well as a much-improved driving experience – albeit only for the five-door. *(Author)*

Power increases weren't confined to the Shogun's diesel line-up, however, as Mitsubishi reckoned there was still the potential to push the Shogun/Pajero even further upmarket. This was achieved in 1994 when a 3497cc 24-valve version of the Shogun V6 was

WHAT THE PRESS SAID:
Shogun 'Series II'

One of the most popular 4x4s in the world, the Shogun has acquired its reputation through extreme toughness and durability off-road. There's a choice of short-wheelbase, three-door body or long-wheelbase, five-door, as well as two tough turbo-diesels and two powerful petrol V6s.

The Express World Car Guide 1999 (Express Newspapers)

announced in both three- and five-door guises, offering a class-leading 205bhp at 5000rpm and a mighty 221lb ft of all-important torque at 3000rpm.

Interestingly, the 3.5-litre wasn't a replacement for the 3.0-litre V6, but was actually an addition to the range and a deliberate ploy to beat the V8-engined Land Rover Discovery in the power stakes. In real terms, this meant an on-the-road top speed (where allowed) of 107mph for the Shogun 3.5 V6 five-door, with the 0–60mph sprint achieved in a previously unheard of (within this class) 10.7 seconds. The three-door was even faster at 116mph and 9.5 seconds respectively; never had a Shogun had so much power to play with.

But never had a Shogun been so thirsty! Interestingly, the 3.5-litre Shogun V6 was only marginally less economical than the 3.0-litre version, a tribute to the advances in engine design through the late 1980s and early '90s. It was still feasible for the driver of a Shogun 3.5 V6 to achieve fuel economy in the mid- to high-teens, as long as he had a reasonably sympathetic right

When the 3.5-litre V6 was introduced in '94, many assumed that the 3.0-litre (shown here) would be discontinued. Instead, Mitsubishi saw the newcomer as an expansion of the range rather than the replacement of an older model. *(Mitsubishi)*

foot and didn't use the automatic's 'kickdown' facility at every opportunity.

Indeed, Series II Shoguns with automatic transmission became increasingly popular, though this option was restricted solely to the V6 right through to the end of 1993. The following year – coinciding with the arrival of the 2.8-litre – was when a turbo-diesel Shogun automatic became available once again.

This applied only to UK-spec Shoguns and the official British line-up of the time. In Japan, most buyers of turbo-diesel Pajeros still opted for automatic transmission, which is why Mitsubishi kept its availability going in its homeland throughout the life of the second-generation version, and also why most of the used diesel-powered Pajeros imported to the UK in recent years have been automatics.

Maybe Mitsubishi didn't believe there was much of a market for a turbo-diesel automatic in the fairly traditional British 4x4 scene of the early 1990s, despite the reasonable success of the first-generation models. Whatever the reason, it's obviously not an issue now for

the thousands of British owners driving round in automatic, imported Pajeros – and quite right too. With the extra power offered in Series II guise, a turbo-diesel Pajero offering impressively smooth automatic gear changes makes for a fairly effortless driving experience.

WHAT THE PRESS SAID: Shogun 'Series II'

If this is your first big 4x4, handling is going to take a while to get used to. Whilst it feels considerably choppier than a car, it's still one of the best in its class. Considering the Shogun's size, there's very little body roll and the steering is both light and responsive. You might even go as far as to describe the short-wheelbase Shogun as nimble.

4x4 Mart, April 2000

Market pressures

The fact that a sub-3.0-litre petrol engine was never made available in the British Shogun line-up of 1991-onwards says a great deal about changing market attitudes. When it came to full-size 4x4s, diesel had rapidly become the logical power choice for buyers of all types of different makes and models, leaving the petrol option only for those seeking the performance of a V6 or even a V8.

Even more crucially, the decision said a lot about Mitsubishi's determination to push the Pajero/Shogun brand ever further upmarket, and the UK pricing strategy of the second-generation Shogun was proof of this. By 1996, for example, the cheapest Shogun 2.8 TD five-door (the GLX) was costing not far short of 20% more than a Land Rover Discovery 2.5 TDi five-door.

At the top of the petrol-engined ranges it was a similar story, with the Shogun 3.5 V6 five-door costing around 25% more than the most expensive Discovery 3.9 V8 ES, simply for the 'privilege' of a V6 engine over a V8. So what was Mitsubishi's reasoning behind this?

Major improvements inside gave the Series II a far more civilised, cosseting feel than its predecessor. Mitsubishi knew the Shogun/Pajero had to be comfortable, well equipped and superbly finished to guarantee success. *(Mitsubishi)*

To put it into context, we should remember that – even as recently as the late 1990s – Britain still had a voluntary 'gentlemen's agreement' restricting the number of Japanese cars sold there. In consequence, an average of no more than 3500 examples of the second-generation Shogun was imported to the UK each year, so Mitsubishi was naturally more interested in selling the upmarket versions with their greater profit margins. It did the Shogun brand a lot of good in the process however, as it was now more than ever seen by the buying public as a genuine Range Rover rival, a step up from the Discovery in terms of pricing, equipment and image. That's why, by 1996, a top-of-the-range Shogun 3.5 V6 was not so much more affordable than a mid-range Range Rover V8 SE. In the UK at least, the Shogun was now more exclusive and more expensive than Mitsubishi's designers had ever originally intended.

It wasn't like this in every market worldwide, as many buyers outside the UK demanded Pajeros they could easily afford to buy and run – the 'workhorses' of the range, if you like. Consequently, some export versions were almost utilitarian in their equipment levels, but when it came to the Pajero's homeland, it was yet another story: as we'll discover in Chapter Five, the Japanese have always liked their Pajeros heavily laden with all kinds of extra equipment and luxury, which is why a Japanese-spec Pajero can often make a British-spec Shogun feel almost basic by comparison.

More style, more goodies

It's all relative, though, as the Shogun really was a well-equipped machine in its own right, helping to give the model a more upmarket image in the UK than ever before; but there was more to the Shogun's upward shift than mere equipment. Mitsubishi knew they couldn't make a silk purse out of a sow's ear, so the latest Shogun/Pajero models had to be more refined,

WHAT THE PRESS SAID:
Shogun 'Series II'

The second-generation Shogun which was introduced in 1991 was a very clever piece of product development. It retained all the strengths of its predecessors, but dressed them up in more aerodynamic and contemporary styling and added improved equipment levels. The package allowed the range to be moved further upmarket in many territories, including the UK...

www.difflock.com

Mitsubishi may have made the most of the Shogun/Pajero's 'country set' image, but this was a truly versatile machine – just as capable of looking good in the company car park as it was coping with the rough stuff off-road. *(Mitsubishi)*

better performing and a more cosseting experience all round if they were to take on the most expensive products from Land Rover.

Fortunately for all concerned, the recipe for the second-generation Shogun/Pajero was spot on, and it didn't take long for Britain's motoring press, in particular, to start heaping praise on the newcomer for offering so many major improvements over its predecessor.

What Car? magazine, summing up every new car available in the UK in its October 1991 issue, praised the Series II Shogun for being '…very civilised inside', going as far as to suggest that the '…smooth diesels and slick gearboxes make [the] Discovery's seem almost crude'. That kind of encouragement from one of Europe's most respected car-buying magazines was enough to get the latest Shogun off to a flying start.

But it didn't end with *What Car?* Even when the Series II Shogun was in its final few weeks on sale in the UK, it was still receiving plenty of praise. In April 2000, when I was editor of *4x4 Mart* magazine, freelance writer Will Shiers commented during a Buying Used feature: 'The newer shape is considerably dearer, but these are far

better all-rounders. A post-1991 Shogun looks equally at home axle deep in mud as it does parked outside the opera'.

As a family-carrying vehicle, the second-generation Shogun/Pajero was a big improvement over the original. There was even more room aboard, not to mention a more attractive, more comfortable interior. The vehicle had lost none of its workmanlike qualities, but it succeeded in making them less obvious to the casual observer thanks to such refinements as electrically adjustable seats and mirrors, electric windows all round and leather upholstery on many versions.

The coil-sprung suspension helped provide a more car-like ride quality, too. The Pajero/Shogun was now far better at soaking up the bumps, going round corners in a hurry and offering a more driver-friendly experience – not least aided by the steady

New flared wheel arches gave the revised Series II range a more dynamic image in 1997. Mitsubishi knew 4x4 buyers were becoming increasingly style conscious, hence this smart facelift six years into the model's nine-year career. *(Mitsubishi)*

improvements in power and performance during its career. It had become just about as sophisticated as any traditional 4x4 with a separate ladder-frame chassis could ever hope to be.

Steady development

It wasn't just the Shogun/Pajero's engines that were upgraded during its nine years on sale. October 1997 brought the most obvious visual alteration of the model's career, when its already handsome appearance was enhanced by the addition of flared wheel arches. These shouldn't be confused with the 'add-on' plastic arches that had been fitted to most 1991–97 models from day one, made all the more obvious when specified as part of a two-tone colour scheme. No, these latest wheel arches gave a more gradual flare to all four corners of the vehicle, cleverly endowing it with a wider, more sophisticated look.

The change seemed subtle in the initial press

photographs supplied by Mitsubishi in 1997, but 'in the flesh' was dramatically more effective. And alongside freshened-up front grilles, a new range of colour options and even more equipment fitted as standard, the result was a useful update for the Series II's final two and a half years on sale.

Yes, as the end of the 20th century hove into view, Mitsubishi was once again busying itself with preparations for the launch of another completely new generation of Shogun/Pajero models. The first-generation line-up had done spectacularly well for eight years, while the next generation had been successful for almost nine. But, as ever, the world's 4x4 markets were developing at a rapid rate, and it was essential for Mitsubishi to stay one step ahead of the game.

Little did the Shogun/Pajero's more traditional buyers realise just what a dramatic change of direction the Series III range would represent.

Even towards the end of the Series II's life, there was never a shortage of Shogun/Pajero customers. But with the new millennium on the horizon, Mitsubishi saw the need for an all-new replacement. The end was nigh. *(Mitsubishi)*

Chapter Three

Super Shogun!

That the Series II Shogun/Pajero was in need of replacement as the new millennium dawned wasn't in dispute. It had, after all, been around for the best part of a decade; and with most of Europe's major manufacturers now joining the 4x4 party in an effort to beat both Land Rover and the Japanese at their own game, the pressure was well and truly on Mitsubishi not to let the Shogun fall behind.

What arrived for the 2000 model year, though, shocked many people. Mitsubishi proudly unveiled its all-new Shogun/Pajero for the 21st century – and for the first time ever, here was a Shogun without a separate chassis.

Most manufacturers of conventional cars switched from a separate-chassis format to monocoque design way back in the 1960s, tempted by the promise of cheaper and simpler production techniques. It meant the cars were generally lighter in weight, and therefore both quicker and more economical. Crucially, their integral strength was now gained via the clever design

Left: Curvaceous new looks and monocoque construction marked a major change of direction for the new Shogun/Pajero of 2000. Would fans of the previous models take to such a radical departure? Many onlookers had their doubts. *(Mitsubishi)*

Below: Mitsubishi were keen to stress the strength, rigidity and off-road prowess of their all-new model, even though it lacked the traditional separate chassis favoured by off-road manufacturers; it was a message they needed to shout very loudly to be heard. *(Mitsubishi)*

of their entire bodyshell and individual body panels rather than any kind of main backbone chassis.

The 4x4 scene had traditionally been different. A sturdy separate chassis had always been considered essential for any serious off-road machine, as it provided the ultimate in structural rigidity and strength – both vital when a vehicle is being pushed to the limit in the most inhospitable terrain. A decent chassis stops a 4x4's body structure from flexing or twisting under pressure, an important requirement of any off-road enthusiast. And now, all of a sudden, Mitsubishi was throwing away the entire concept and going along the monocoque route; but why?

Out with the old

Well, in some ways it was a logical decision. Monocoque-designed vehicles have always offered a smoother on-road ride, superior handling and better

The proof of the pudding? Despite the fears of more traditional buyers, the latest-generation Shogun/Pajero proved a capable contender in the rough. The biggest problem was the massive rear overhang of the five-door model. *(Mitsubishi)*

all-round refinement than a 4x4 with a separate chassis, and with most purchasers of upmarket Shoguns having them primarily for tarmac use by the end of the 1990s, such considerations were higher up Mitsubishi's list of priorities than they had been in the early 1980s.

Even so, many traditionalists threw up their hands in horror. The Shogun/Pajero had often been viewed by fans worldwide as a hard-working 4x4 first and foremost, with its increasingly upmarket image and its fashionable status being of less importance in many cases. But now, it was feared, Mitsubishi was effectively saying: 'Too bad, we're looking after the tarmac dwellers from now on'.

Happily, despite the modern approach of a monocoque design, the new-for-2000 Shogun/Pajero still proved to be something of an accomplished off-roader – albeit with a few compromises, which we'll deal with later. So those people who decried the company's brave design decision to begin with were often satisfied with what they found once they got behind the wheel.

Just how different was the newcomer compared with the Shogun/Pajeros of old, and was the 4x4 market ready for a vehicle that looked so surprisingly unusual?

Brave new world

The third-generation Shogun/Pajero was the least conventional 4x4 from Mitsubishi that the world had seen – and it all started with its unusual, curvaceous, almost sensual styling. Where most 4x4s were tall, boxy affairs, the all-new Shogun offered sweeping curves, daring bulges and an on-road presence that screamed DON'T IGNORE ME at every other road user. It was a brave move.

There was no ignoring the latest big 4x4 from Mitsubishi. From any angle, this all-new machine couldn't possibly be mistaken for any of its rivals. As before, three-door short-wheelbase and five-door long-wheelbase versions would become available. *(Mitsubishi)*

As before, the new range was available in a choice of short- or long-wheelbase guises with three and five doors respectively. Whichever model was chosen, it shared the same level of curvaceousness and similar attention-grabbing styling cues – despite a considerable 20 inches difference in overall length. Whatever your favourite from the new line-up, you couldn't accuse Mitsubishi of missing out on a dramatic restyling opportunity!

A similar theme continued inside the new Shogun/Pajero, where the dashboard was modern, stylish and extremely well laid out. Gone was the designed-for-working interior of the original Shogun; here was an upmarket 4x4 created for those with a sense of style rather than an urgent need to haul dead sheep around.

You deduce this from the various user-friendly and

Never before had a Shogun or Pajero been so luxurious! The interior of the latest version was a world away from the utilitarian approach of 17 years earlier. Standard equipment levels were generous, to say the least. *(Author)*

How's this for a neat touch? The third row of seats in the five-door model could be stowed flat under the floor when not in use, instead of taking up valuable luggage space as before. Convenience was now a major selling point. *(Mitsubishi)*

neat touches on board, not least the rearmost accommodation in the seven-seater long-wheelbase model. Mitsubishi had given this a great deal of thought, finally doing away with the individual seats for

WHAT THE PRESS SAID:
Shogun 3.2 TD Di-D Equippe three-door

Bulging wheelarches and racy spoilers appeal to the boy-racer enthusiast, while legendary reliability makes this the favourite of many otherwise quite conservative families. Either way, the Shogun has established itself as a key rival to the all-conquering Land Rovers, offering good equipment and comfortable accommodation at a reasonably accessible price.

4x4 magazine, November 2002

people six and seven at the back. Instead there was now a bench seat that, when not in use, folded down into the floor rather than up the sides of the luggage area. The result was greater boot space and a wide, completely flat loadspace. It was a neatly engineered touch, instantly giving the new Shogun/Pajero a head start against the Land Rover Discovery in the best-for-large-families stakes.

In typical Shogun/Pajero style, the newcomers were also rather well equipped – as they should be, given their higher-than-ever pricing strategy. In 2000, British buyers of a brand-new Shogun would have spent little less on a 3.5 GDI V6 GLS five-door automatic than they would have done on a 4.0-litre V8-engined Range Rover County.

No wonder Mitsubishi felt obliged to equip that version with just about every modern convenience imaginable. All except for traction control, that is – a major failing in many onlookers' eyes, given the fact that tempting new rivals like the Mercedes-Benz M-Class and even the heavily-revised Discovery were including this as standard.

Under the body

The Shogun/Pajero's break with tradition was, it has to be said, kept mainly to its use of monocoque construction and its adventurous body styling. Beneath the bodywork things were relatively straightforward, albeit greatly improved over the old-style models.

For a start, there was a new range of petrol and diesel engines – and Mitsubishi was making great claims about their capabilities. The smallest capacity available in the UK was a 3200cc direct-injection turbo diesel, a powerful and torquey unit offering 162bhp (at 3800rpm) and 275lb ft (at just 2000rpm). That was enough for an on-road top speed (should it be allowed) of 99mph, with 60mph being reached from rest in under than 13 seconds for the long-wheelbase version. For a big, heavy 4x4 (not far off 16 feet in overall length), these were very respectable achievements, particularly when compared with the rather sluggish diesel-powered Shoguns of old.

But what exactly were the advantages of a direct-injection diesel engine, a term being talked about a great deal at the start of the new century? According to Mitsubishi, it was all perfectly logical: 'Fuel is injected at high pressure directly into the engine's combustion chamber, whilst the induction port is designed to cause air to 'swirl' on intake. This turbulence causes the fuel

Shoguns have always excelled in tough, off-road terrain – though Mitsubishi openly admitted that on-road dynamics were more important than off-road prowess when they went the monocoque route. That said, this latest version is still a damn fine off-road machine, with shift-on-the-fly operation of its dual-range transfer box – plus the usefulness of a '4LLc' setting which locks the differentials (centre and rear) for when the going gets really tough. The end result is a luxury SUV that's capable of powering its way through some pretty impressive terrain.

4x4 Mart, October 2003

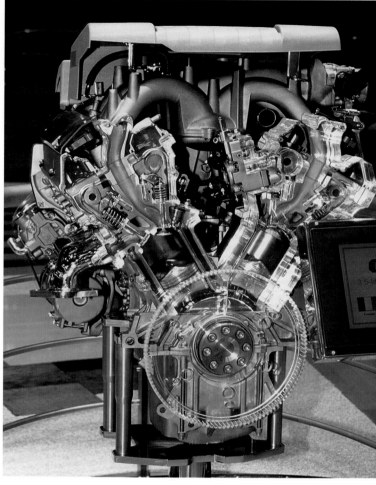

Under the bonnet of the new Shogun/Pajero sat Gasoline Direct Injection (GDI) technology, another headline-grabbing first for Mitsubishi. It resulted in a range of flexible and – for their size – economical powerplants. *(Mitsubishi)*

and air to mix completely and vaporise instantly. As the piston rises, it creates compression 'swirl' resulting in more efficient combustion which benefits economy, power and emissions by eliminating the heat losses and negative workload found in more conventional engines with a separate swirl chamber.' So now you know.

Mitsubishi, though, wasn't content with saving direct-injection technology purely for its diesel-engine range. It wanted to go one step further, adapting the system for the Shogun's new V6 powerplant, too. That's why modern-day petrol-engined Mitsubishis are so often seen bearing the initials 'GDI', which can confuse the casual observer into thinking they're diesel-powered. In reality though, 'GDI' refers to Gasoline Direct Injection, a feature Mitsubishi was keen to explain: 'The secret of GDI technology is this ability to have variable fuel injection timing, a feature which makes the engine efficient in all load conditions: when dealing with less load, it operates in Ultra-Lean combustion mode, where compression stroke injection creates a stratified air-fuel mixture. In higher load operation the engine switches to Superior Output mode with injection on the induction stroke.

To achieve the powerful low-end torque figures, the GDI temporarily switches to two-stage mixing where an ultra-lean knock-suppression spray of fuel is injected during the induction stroke, creating a stratified mixture with an air/fuel ratio of 60:1. This cools the air entering the cylinders, preventing detonation. An additional injection of fuel on the compression stroke corrects the air/fuel ratio for combustion to take place.'

The figures certainly seemed to add up. The Shogun's new 3.5-litre GDI V6 produced an impressive 200bhp at

5000rpm and 235lb ft of torque at 4000rpm. A flat torque curve ensured decent performance throughout its rev range, but the real benefit lay at lower engine speeds, with the new engine delivering nearly 80 per cent of its maximum torque at a mere 1500rpm – an exceptional achievement from a petrol engine and potentially of great benefit off-road.

As far as the UK market was concerned, this twosome was the only engine choice available in the all-new Shogun line-up. But for other crucial markets – including the Pajero's homeland of Japan – a 3.0-litre petrol engine option was also available, sharing a similar 24-valve V6 layout to the 3.5-litre unit but, as you'd expect, with less power on tap. It filled a useful niche in the market, but one that Mitsubishi evidently felt wasn't large enough for British sales.

The clever new 4x4 set-up was still part-time, but offered a total of three different all-wheel-drive settings: 4H, 4HLc and 4LLc gave the driver an impressive amount of choice when the time came to head away from the tarmac. *(Mitsubishi)*

All-wheel drive

Like all previous Shoguns and Pajeros, the latest 21st century models offered part-time four-wheel drive only. That's where any real similarities between the all-wheel-drive system of the old and new models ended, for Mitsubishi's latest efforts were truly hi-tech, thanks to a major redevelopment of the previous Super Select set-up.

In fact, by 2004 the whole system had evolved even further into what's now known as SS4-II Super Select, though the principles are very similar to those of the 2000-onwards design.

In 2H mode, with just the rear wheels driving, the Shogun/Pajero does exactly what you'd expect it to do – that bit is straightforward enough. At the heart of SS4-

II, though, is a centre differential which distributes power as a 33/67 per cent split front-to-rear when the 4H (four-wheel-drive high-ratio) setting is then chosen. However, if the speed difference between the front and rear wheels increases, a VCU automatically operates to limit the action of the centre differential, altering the torque split up to 50/50 per cent.

WHAT THE PRESS SAID:
Shogun 3.2 TD Di-D Classic five-door

One of the most recent converts (to lifestyle 4x4s) is the latest Mitsubishi Shogun. A decade ago the Japanese 4x4 was looked upon as a Land Rover minus the gremlins, but the new version is more like a luxury four-wheel drive estate. Instead of a separate chassis, there's a car-like body welded together from pressed panels. Stout reinforcements have been built in to lend it the extra strength necessary for owners who do intend to venture into the wilds.

What Car? magazine, November 2000

The next setting on the transfer box is 4HLc, offering high-range gearing but with the VCU locked to provide traction on low-grip surfaces like snow or sand. It's a useful setting and, like 4H, can be selected at any speed up to 100km/h (62mph).

For even greater off-road action, you'll need to select 4LLc – which can be done only when the vehicle is at a standstill. This offers low-ratio gearing with the VCU locked, providing the ultimate in all-wheel grip for extreme situations. The locked centre differential sends torque forward, bypassing the VCU, via a high–low transfer counter gear, diff lock hub and a linked plate chain. The transfer gear ratio of 1.9:1 is almost twice that of 4HLc mode, allowing the Shogun/Pajero to deal with genuinely challenging terrain.

I have to say, the whole thing does work well, whether five-speed manual or the popular five-speed automatic (with Sports mode) transmission is specified. The 21st century Shogun/Pajero may have made the compromise of using monocoque construction, but its capabilities in the rough are still vastly greater than most owners will ever need.

Press reaction

Britain's motoring press generally agreed from the start that the new Shogun's technically advanced all-wheel-drive system did work effectively. But there's more to successful off-roading than mere grip, as I pointed out

The more upmarket a 4x4, the less it tends to be used in earnest off-road. In that sense, the 2000-on Shogun/Pajero offered rough-stuff capabilities far in excess of what most potential buyers would realistically need. *(Author)*

Not every member of Britain's motoring press has been impressed with the 2000-onward Shogun's off-road capabilities. With a 4x4 as upmarket as this, however, there has to be a degree of on- and off-road compromise. *(Mitsubishi)*

By the end of 2000, the new entry-level Shogun Classic had joined the British line-up in an effort to extend the range to a broader spread of potential customers. It meant a pricing structure more in line with the latest Land Rover Discovery's. *(Mitsubishi)*

in *4x4 Mart* magazine in October 2003, after testing a Shogun Classic long-wheelbase turbo diesel: '…this latest version is still a damn fine off-road machine, with shift-on-the-fly operation of its dual-range transfer box – plus the usefulness of a '4LLC' setting which locks the differentials (centre and rear) for when the going gets really tough. The end result is a luxury SUV that's capable of powering its way through some pretty impressive terrain. The main downside to serious off-roading is the Shogun five-door's long rear overhang, which obviously limits departure angles and runs the risk of getting caught when tackling particularly steep slopes.'

Much depends on exactly what you demand from your all-wheel-drive machine. Perhaps some testers have different expectations? Maybe; which might explain *4x4* magazine's reaction, in its November 2002 issue, to the Shogun Equippe five-door turbo diesel, all

part of its '4x4 Of The Year' contest: 'In spite of its unnecessarily complex selectable four-wheel-drive system, the Shogun doesn't impress off-road – the lack of axle articulation and heavy rear overhang quickly limit its progress over rough terrain, but it's well built and feels solid and stable when thrashed along a dirt trail.'

So who was right? To be honest, I think both magazines were. There are, of course, far superior off-road machines to the 2000-on Shogun/Pajero; but for what most owners expect from a brand-new £30,000-plus 4x4 in terms of rough-stuff action, it does a good enough job. The problem is, several rivals that have appeared since then – including the impressive Volkswagen Touareg, to name just one – do it even better.

All this could be forgiven, of course, if the third-generation Shogun was the finest 4x4 on the tarmac, but even as far back as November 2000, *What Car?* magazine was thinking otherwise when it pitched a Shogun 3.2 Di-D Classic five-door against a Land Rover Discovery Td5 GS and a Mercedes-Benz ML270 CDi. Despite the Shogun being the only one of the three to

Changes afoot

In typical Mitsubishi style, this Japanese company wasn't about to start resting on its laurels. By the end of the latest Shogun's debut year in the UK, a new entry-level version had joined the range in the shape of the Classic. Offering less equipment than the existing GLX and GLS models (soon to be re-branded Equippe and Elegance respectively as part of a general tidying-up exercise), it meant a more competitive list price and a greater chance of keeping the competition from Solihull in check.

The biggest changes of all though, came in 2003 when the Shogun/Pajero was given a bit of a makeover. Most noticeable was a modified front end, with new lights and front grille endowing the Shogun with a subtly different look. Also, the 'fluting' that used to run up the side of the Shogun's bodywork was now removed for a cleaner, simpler appearance. And the finishing touch, aesthetically, was a set of new-look six-spoke alloys fitted as standard, the whole combination coming together to create a noticeable and very pleasing mini-facelift.

Despite looking fresher than before, the latest

offer the supposed on-road advantages of monocoque construction, the testers had no hesitation in placing it third in the group: 'The Mitsubishi is ruled out by its woeful refinement and feeble cornering ability.'

Those may have been harsh words, but it did underline the fact that, no sooner had the Series III Shogun gone on sale at the start of 2000, than the competition moved another step ahead. Such newcomers as the BMW X5, Lexus RX300 and the forthcoming Series II Discovery were going to give the all-new Shogun a hard time.

British sales of the third-generation Shogun have increased steadily since the model's introduction. The five-door Shogun is shown here alongside a five-door Shogun Pinin as part of a joint advertising campaign in 2001. *(Mitsubishi)*

SIZE DOESN'T MATTER.

By 2004, the Shogun range comprised Classic, Equippe and Warrior versions. Shown here is a fully-loaded Warrior 3.2 TD DI-D which, despite its high equipment levels, actually cost less brand new than its Series II equivalent. *(Mitsubishi)*

Shogun/Pajero was still criticised in some quarters for its less than perfect cornering characteristics, its over-light power-assisted steering and its general lack of refinement – which was a great shame, as it certainly had a great deal going for it. As with the general car market, it seemed to be the 4x4s with prestige badges, such as BMW and Mercedes-Benz, that were winning favour with large numbers of converts.

That didn't stop the third-generation Shogun/Pajero from enjoying healthy sales successes – particularly in the UK. In 2000, while supplies of the all-new Shogun were still fairly limited, British buyers snapped up 1,590 examples. Two years later this had risen to annual UK Shogun sales of 4,166, and an even healthier 4,972 by 2003. Things were still looking good for European and UK Shogun/Pajero sales in 2004, but Mitsubishi wasn't taking any chances.

So, in 2004, another round of revisions came into

force, despite UK Shogun sales having increased by a massive 46 per cent during the first six months of the year. Thirteen different variations were now on sale, still comprising 3.2-litre direct-injection turbo-diesel and 3.5-litre V6 petrol powerplants in a choice of long- or short-wheelbase body styles and a variety of trim levels. By now, the different types were grouped under the Classic, Equippe and Warrior variations – the latter having started out as a limited edition, but finally adopted as a permanent member of the range.

Under pressure from so many other manufacturers and importers, Mitsubishi's UK prices had taken a downward turn since the start of the new millennium, bringing them roughly in line with those in the rest of Europe. Hence, by 2004, the entry-level Shogun 3.2 Di-D Classic three-door was now very competitively priced, while a top-of-the-range 3.5 V6 Warrior five-door was costing substantially less than the most expensive old-model Shogun V6 had done eight years earlier! It wasn't that the Shogun was suddenly starting to creep further downmarket; far from it. This was more a case of bowing to increased market pressure and

tougher than ever competition from some very prestigious brands.

Despite its competitive pricing, the 2004-model Shogun was a very well-equipped vehicle, with even the cheapest short-wheelbase Classic boasting ABS with Electronic Brake-force Distribution (EBD), air conditioning, twin airbags, alloy wheels, central locking, electrically-adjustable door mirrors, side airbags, an alarm, climate control and roof bars. And remember, this was for a brand-new Shogun that now suddenly found itself costing even less (just about) than a top-of-the-range Land Rover Freelander three-door. Value for money was very much back on the Shogun/Pajero agenda.

Perhaps the most important change of all for 2004 was the adoption across the Shogun range of traction control, known officially as M-ASTC – Mitsubishi Active Stability & Traction Control System. The criticisms of *What Car?* (and others) had finally been answered, and the Shogun was now much closer to being on a par with its rivals from BMW, Mercedes-Benz, Jeep and Land Rover.

The 2005-model UK-spec Shoguns also came in for an array of changes to keep interest in the range high.

If you think all four-wheel-drive police vehicles are Land Rovers or Range Rovers, think again. The Series III has caught on with several forces in recent years, combining long-term reliability with excellent value for money. *(Mitsubishi)*

Prices were 'realigned' (mostly reduced) yet again, and the line-up was expanded slightly to ensure all potential customers could find a Shogun to suit their needs; for example, the option of five-speed manual transmission was offered on long-wheelbase models, where automatic had previously been the only choice.

The early years of the 21st century were particularly tough for Mitsubishi, with sales across its extensive range plunging in Japan and even in some parts of Europe. But the one bright spot through all the financial difficulties was the third-generation Shogun/Pajero, which managed to maintain its sales far more successfully than most other models from Mitsubishi. The vehicle may not have been perfect, but its general competence, its value for money and its maker's unspoiled reputation for unbeatable reliability stood it in good stead. The Shogun and Pajero were – and still are – very much alive and kicking.

Chapter Four

Family likeness

The worldwide success of the Shogun/Pajero since the unveiling of the original versions in 1982 understandably led Mitsubishi to look at other areas of the 4x4 market. After all, if the company could succeed in one sector of the all-wheel-drive scene, why couldn't this success be repeated elsewhere?

Happily, most of these resulting new 4x4s have made it to Europe – and elsewhere – in the intervening years, enabling Mitsubishi fans the world over to enjoy a wide range of alternative models. A rare exception to this is the Pajero Junior, a miniature (Suzuki Jimny-sized) 4x4 designed primarily for Japanese consumption because of various tax laws which penalise larger vehicles. Looking like a seriously scaled-down Series I Pajero,

Mitsubishi's expertise in the 4x4 market isn't confined merely to off-roaders. You have only to look at the amazing success of various generations of rally-winning EVO models to appreciate this.

(Mitsubishi)

the Junior achieved almost cult status in its native Japan but is generally not well known elsewhere. A very small number have been personally imported to the UK over the years, but they're just about as 'niche' as any Mitsubishi 4x4 can be – which is why we won't be going into any great detail about them here.

There are other all-wheel-drive Mitsubishis not officially available in the UK which I will be covering in this chapter, because of their close relationship with the Shoguns and Pajeros we're familiar with, as well as the fact that large numbers have made it to British shores thanks to the efforts of many enterprising importers of used cars.

Mitsubishi's expertise in the 4x4 market isn't confined to off-roaders or SUVs, of course. There is also the legendary all-wheel-drive Lancer EVO, the ultimate model of which – at the time of writing – has to be the EVO VIII of 2005. But, for obvious reasons, I'm not going to use up valuable space in a Shogun/Pajero book on a rally-winning saloon car, fascinating though it may be.

Far more relevant to us are the following Mitsubishi 4x4s, all in some way linked with the world-beater that is Shogun and Pajero:

L200

The history of the Mitsubishi L200 pick-up range goes right back to the 1970s when, as a boxy but incredibly robust one-tonne truck, this newcomer found itself on the receiving end of praise the world over. It even caught the attention of critics in America, the world's biggest market for pick-up trucks, where it received the accolade of 'USA Pick-Up of the Year' in 1979.

An all-new L200 range was introduced in 1987, and survived a whole decade before being usurped by yet another new truck of the same name. It is this L200 of

Above: The Mitsubishi L200 has been the best-selling truck in its class for many years, with sales of the various double-cab versions being particularly buoyant. This 1999 example was put through its paces by the author for *4x4 Mart* magazine. *(Author)*

Below: Whether in two- or four-wheel-drive guises, the L200 has an unrivalled reputation for reliability, longevity and an ability to thrive on abuse. No wonder it has managed to stave off competition from so many rivals over the years. *(Mitsubishi)*

1997 onwards that has seen the most spectacular success, particularly in the UK where sales have exploded at an unprecedented rate. Indeed, by the early years of the 21st century, the L200 was the best-selling Mitsubishi imported to the UK, outselling every passenger car and 4x4 range offered by the company.

This is all well and good, of course, but what's it got

The big expansion in L200 sales over the years has been in the leisure market, with fully-loaded versions like the Animal Cab proving a tempting and tax-efficient alternative to the 4x4s and more conventional SUVs. *(Mitsubishi)*

to do with the history of the Shogun and Pajero? More than you might think, because the L200 provided a lot of the design and technical inspiration behind the original Pajero, and the L200 4x4 also has more than a bit in common with what we now know in the UK as the Shogun Sport (elsewhere as the Challenger).

So why is it that the 1997-onwards L200 has been so massively successful? Partly because it's always been seen as one of the most durable, hard-working vehicles in its class, as well as offering a finer new-vehicle warranty than any rival. But it's not just the L200's capabilities that have guaranteed its success; it's also happily benefited from a major shift within the truck market and from a useful change in the UK's company car tax and VAT rules.

The demise of Ford's Sierra-based P100 pick-up was a major loss to the one-tonne truck market, as this had traditionally been the best-seller in Britain. But it gave Mitsubishi a major advantage; and when the all-new L200 arrived in 1997, the company had every intention of exploiting the situation.

The new L200 was a major step forward from its predecessor of the same name, offering a far more car-like driving experience as well as fresh, modern styling. It looked smarter and drove better than the Toyota Hilux, Nissan Pick-Up and Vauxhall Brava of the time (all of which were getting on in years), and it was

among the most reliable, most dependable vehicles on the road.

The start of the 21st century saw the British government giving the pick-up market a major boost when it changed the rules for VAT and company car tax on double-cab trucks. It meant that as long as a four- or five-seater double-cab offered a payload of at least one tonne, it would be classed as a commercial vehicle rather than a passenger car (as it had been before). Consequently, any VAT-registered buyer of an L200 double-cab could now reclaim 17.5 per cent of its purchase price; and anybody opting for an L200 double-cab as a company vehicle would pay a minuscule amount in tax compared with that on a 'normal' company car.

Such changes brought a massive boost to Britain's pick-up scene, with potential buyers now seeing the advantages of a low-tax vehicle capable of carrying five people and a serious number of personal belongings. Suddenly, double-cab four-wheel-drive trucks were being viewed as viable alternatives to the more conventional 4x4s of the time.

Never one to miss an opportunity, Mitsubishi set about expanding its L200 line-up, offering a choice of rear- and four-wheel-drive, single- and double-cab trucks. But it was the double-cab 4x4 L200s that really got the sector excited, particularly once models aimed unashamedly at the 'leisure' market started arriving.

Model names like 4Life and Warrior became part of the L200 line-up, offering a Shogun-based all-wheel-drive set-up (with dual-range transfer box), ex-Shogun 2.5-litre turbo-diesel powerplant and a whole range of on-board goodies as standard equipment. Mitsubishi even experimented with bringing over a limited number of 3.0-litre V6-engined L200s, but the prohibitive fuel consumption and heftier running costs deterred most buyers, and this model – known as the Triton – soon disappeared.

Even so, the L200 went from strength to strength. In 1998, Mitsubishi achieved annual L200 sales in Britain of just 1600 units; by 2003 this had boomed to an astonishing 12,574, representing the largest percentage increase of any mass-produced vehicle on sale in the UK during that time. It was an incredible result.

The technology used in today's L200, of course, is broadly like that employed in previous-generation Shoguns and Pajeros, with similar engines, similar 4x4 systems and similar separate-chassis design. That's why, in some ways, an L200 4x4 double-cab answers the needs of anybody interested in a new, old-style

How was this for a brave idea? Mitsubishi fitted their 3.0-litre V6 petrol engine in the L200 at one stage, creating the awesomely powerful (by truck standards) Triton model. Sadly, its sales success in the UK was less than spectacular. *(Author)*

Shogun/Pajero parked on their driveway. Or they could, of course, just go out and buy a Shogun Sport instead.

Challenger/Shogun Sport

Even before the all-new monocoque-design, third-generation Shogun/Pajero was unveiled for the 2000 model year, Mitsubishi could see a gap in the market for a more straightforward, more traditional family-sized 4x4. That's why, for 1998, along came the Challenger – renamed Shogun Sport for the UK market just two years later. But if the new Challenger

WHAT THE PRESS SAID: Challenger

The Challenger is a new hybrid from Mitsubishi, combining the chassis of the Shogun with the front of the L200 pick-up and a new five-door estate body behind. By cutting down on the costly construction of the Shogun, a whole new sector of more budget-conscious buyers has been targeted.

The Express World Car Guide 1999 (Express Newspapers)

Derived from the L200, the new Mitsubishi Challenger was a useful addition to Mitsubishi's 4x4 line-up. Undercutting the Shogun on price, it offered the advantages of a traditional SUV for those on a tighter budget. (Mitsubishi)

With a choice of 2.5-litre turbo-diesel or 3.0-litre V6 petrol power, the Challenger's engine line-up was predictable. In fact, its entire specification lacked any major surprises, much to the delight of fans of older-style Shoguns and Pajeros. (Author)

looked somehow familiar from certain angles, this was no surprise.

The Challenger was quite intentionally based around the L200 of 1997-onwards. Look at the front-end styling – the front doors, the wings, the bonnet. They're all reminiscent of the L200, because they're all basically borrowed from the L200's parts bin. In fact, in simple terms, the Challenger was the front end and chassis of an L200 with a long, estate-like body grafted on the rear. It was a relatively affordable way of creating a five-door all-wheel-drive SUV, as it avoided the exorbitant expense of designing a new model from scratch.

It wasn't all good news, of course. Being based on a pick-up truck, the Challenger soon found itself criticised for its harsh ride, choppy handling and lack of in-built refinement. But such criticisms were cruel in many ways, for the Challenger had a great deal going for it – not least its value for money and its sheer unburstable nature.

Any SUV that's derived directly from a truck is going to feel slightly agricultural compared with the latest in bespoke 4x4 designs. The Hilux-based Toyota Surf was proof of that, and the Challenger was no exception. On the other hand, truck-based SUVs tend to be extremely roomy, as they have a far longer passenger and luggage area than most rivals.

Even inside the Challenger, there was evidence of the L200 in the dashboard and fascia design. But from there back, it was a refreshing experience, aided by Mitsubishi's loading of the newcomer with just about every mod con and electrical gizmo most buyers might want.

Under the bonnet of the Challenger sat the familiar 2.5-litre turbo-diesel four-cylinder unit, albeit with an intercooler to match the power of the similar-engined Series II Shogun/Pajero. Those with a thirst for thirstiness could opt for Mitsubishi's well-known 3.0-litre V6, a model understandably less popular in Europe where sales of diesel cars have escalated in recent years.

So just where in the Mitsubishi range did the Challenger sit? Directly below the Shogun is the logical answer. In 1999, for example (the Series II Shogun's last year on sale), a British-spec Challenger 2.5 GLX turbo-diesel cost a little under 20 per cent less than the cheapest five-door Shogun, the 2.8 GLX. You could buy a Shogun for the same price as a Challenger, but it would be a three-door, short-wheelbase model with, inevitably, less room, less boot space and fewer doors.

It was a similar story at the top of the Challenger line-up, with the most expensive 3.0 V6 GLS being pitched, competitively, at 16–17 per cent less than a five-door Shogun of the same trim level. That important price difference between models meant there was virtually no overlap between the Challenger and Shogun ranges, as well as some useful extra 4x4 sales for Mitsubishi each year.

Being unashamedly truck-based, the Challenger didn't have the same kind of upmarket image as the Shogun, or indeed the same following amongst the 'sub-Range Rover' set. But for 4x4 buyers whose budgets would have been overstretched by a brand new Shogun, it was an important offering.

You might think that the launch of the all-new Series III Shogun/Pajero in 2000 would have made the

WHAT THE PRESS SAID: Challenger

Wine connoisseurs often tell us that some wines get better with age. Well, the same can be said about some cars. Mitsubishi's Challenger is one of them.

The Australian, October 12th 2000

Challenger seem even more outmoded, in both looks and specification. But this wasn't the case. In fact, because the latest vehicle to wear a Shogun or Pajero badge was so unconventional by 4x4 standards, the Challenger suddenly seemed to make even more sense for those who hankered after an 'old school' Shogun.

Mitsubishi realised this. They also realised that bringing the two ranges closer together – in name at least – would benefit them both. And so, from 2000, the Challenger was renamed Shogun Sport, albeit only in the UK. It formed one third of an all-new Shogun line-up, which would also include the new Shogun Pinin 'mini 4x4'.

The Shogun Sport was essentially the same as the Challenger in all but very minor details, and has since gone on to achieve some success. In the UK in 2003, a total of 1830 Shogun Sports found buyers compared with 1927 the previous year. By 2004 though, Shogun Sport sales were taking off in Britain, following a significant price reduction that year which resulted in the entry-level 2.5 TD Classic being something of a bargain. Indeed, in the first six months of 2004,

The change of name from Challenger to Shogun Sport was a logical move, particularly given the forthcoming launch of the tiny Shogun Pinin. The Shogun family would soon comprise three separate model ranges, a first for Mitsubishi. *(Author)*

WHAT THE PRESS SAID:
Shogun Pinin 2.0 five-door

The Pinin is a clever enough concept but, as so often happens with such compact designs, the effort to pack five seats and useful luggage space into a small bodyshell results in rather cramped accommodation and uninteresting, boxy styling. The Pinin's neat lines give it a fair amount of high street presence and it doesn't look out of place in the rough, but it would be stretching a point to say it was a beautiful or charismatic car.

4x4 magazine, November 2002

Mitsubishi sold substantially more Shogun Sports than they managed in the whole of 2003.

Even so, these aren't huge totals, but the Shogun Sport has proved a useful addition to the Shogun family – and a couple-or-more-thousand extra sales a year for Mitsubishi's British operations has certainly been a welcome boost.

Shogun Pinin

Even with the Shogun Sport filling the gap just below the Shogun/Pajero line-up, Mitsubishi knew it was still missing out on the biggest sector of the new millennium's ever-expanding 4x4 scene: the 'compact' market. Yes, if you'd gone looking in Mitsubishi's

corporate cupboard for a Land Rover Freelander, Suzuki Grand Vitara or Toyota RAV4 rival at the end of 1999, you'd have found it well and truly bare.

Enter the Shogun/Pajero Pinin, the company's new-for-2000 'mini 4x4' aimed at attracting a younger, less affluent audience. Catch them while they're young, went the argument, and you might hang on to them when they want a bigger 4x4. It was a plausible theory, even if the Pinin's European sales success has been rather mediocre in the ensuing years.

As with the RAV4, it was the short-wheelbase three-door Shogun Pinin that seemed to offer the greater charisma, while the longer-wheelbase five-door version (introduced in 2001) was the more sensible choice. Even so, neither model seemed to offer the same kind of characterful styling as its major rivals.

Under the skin, things were competent enough thanks to coil-sprung suspension, a choice of 1.8- and 2.0-litre petrol (GDI) power and, of course, four-wheel drive. Rather confusingly though, some Pinin versions over the years have used permanent all-wheel drive (a Shogun/Pajero first), aided by a VCU which provides 50/50 torque distribution between the front and rear wheels, while others have employed a part-time system going by the name of SS4-i.

In many ways, SS4-i mirrors the set-up used in the Series III Shogun/Pajero, offering a choice of 2H, 4H, 4HLc

Making its debut at the Geneva Motor Show, the diminutive Shogun Pinin three-door was Mitsubishi's attempt to cash in on some of Suzuki's mini-4x4 market dominance. Chunky styling and terrific value for money attracted plenty of attention. *(Mitsubishi)*

and 4LLc settings. The ideal use for each setting is pretty obvious, with 4H being the most popular all-wheel-drive option for on-road driving during poor weather conditions or even for a spot of minor off-roading.

Thanks to reasonable ground clearance, short overhangs front and rear and, in the case of SS4-i, an all-wheel-drive system intended for the rough stuff, a

The arrival of the five-door Shogun/Pajero Pinin extended Mitsubishi's 4x4 range still further, though sales of the Pinin line-up have hardly set the SUV scene alight. With its longer wheelbase, the five-door is the most sensible choice. *(Mitsubishi)*

Take a Shogun/Pajero Pinin off-road and you might be surprised by its capabilities. Despite its low pricing and its fairly lacklustre image, this is one of the most competent tiny 4x4s you're likely to come across in the rough. *(Mitsubishi)*

It doesn't have the most exciting interior around, but the Pinin is well designed inside and reasonably comfortable on all but the longest journeys. Shown here is a Pinin 2.0 GDI with optional automatic transmission. *(Mitsubishi)*

Shogun/Pajero Pinin can be fairly accomplished off-road. In fact, Britain's *4x4* magazine was impressed when it put a five-door Pinin 2.0 through its paces as part of its '4x4 Of The Year 2003' contest, commenting: '…the true off-road drive train with low range gearing gives it quite impressive off-road ability, so it has much dynamic appeal.'

The long-wheelbase Pinin was the model of choice when it came to on-road handling, too. In my experience, no standard Pinin will ever go round a corner with quite the same level of confidence and ability as a Toyota RAV4, but the five-door model is still a fairly neat handler. By comparison, the three-door short-wheelbase feels skittish and almost scary at times – until you get used to it, anyway.

The Pinin had a major ace up its sleeve when it first went on sale: its sheer value for money. As the years went on, this was not only maintained but – as with other more recent Shoguns – actually improved upon.

Despite keen prices, the Shogun Pinin hasn't been a massive success in Britain, and it hasn't fared much better in mainland Europe. In 2001, the first full year of three-door and five-door Pinin sales, a total of 3728 examples found British buyers. Two years later though, this annual total had dropped to a mere 1933 Pinins.

Was the market to blame? No, because sales of

'compact' 4x4s have boomed in recent years, with major rival Suzuki posting particularly healthy 4x4 sales increases since the Pinin has been around. Perhaps Mitsubishi doesn't promote the model sufficiently, or maybe it's just not trendy enough for today's youngest 4x4 buyers. Whatever the reason, it's a shame. Anybody who dismisses the Pinin without at least trying it first could be missing out on a real value-for-money alternative to the better-selling small 4x4s out there.

Delica Space Gear

At least British customers get a chance to buy a Pinin if they want to, though. The same luxury has never been

WHAT THE PRESS SAID: Delica Space Gear

...those vehicle manufacturers that think they know best reckon not enough Brits would buy an off-road MPV. But I think they're wrong. These days, plenty of folk like to carry their extended family and friends with them when they're out and about at weekends; and many of us also have the kinds of hobbies that involve either groups of other people or lots of equipment. Having a vehicle that would carry the most challenging of passenger/equipment combinations whilst also offering all-wheel drive for extra convenience ... well, I reckon it could do pretty well. Boating enthusiasts; sports-mad families; caravanners ... you name them, I think they'd take to the idea of an off-road MPV.

4x4 Mart, October 2004

extended to the hugely successful Delica Space Gear, an all-wheel-drive MPV with more than a passing link with the older Shoguns and Pajeros.

The Delica name actually goes way back to 1968, when Mitsubishi launched a half-ton pick-up truck going by that very moniker. Van and passenger-carrying versions arrived in 1969, but it wasn't until a decade later that the first four-wheel-drive Delica was let loose in Japan – a go-anywhere version of the van we knew in Britain (in two-wheel-drive guise) as the L300.

The Delica we're most concerned about here, though – officially known as the Delica Space Gear – wasn't launched until 1994, and it was a major step forward

Yes, that really is an official badge on the side of a top-of-the-range Delica Space Gear Jasper. Mitsubishi obviously wanted to stress why the Space Gear was essential for your lifestyle, hence this rather bizarre sticker! *(Author)*

for the model. This was the least van-like of all Delicas to date; and was the model that really mastered the art of mixing an MPV with an all-wheel-drive off-roader.

The Delica Space Gear's roots are unashamedly van-based. In fact, the van version of the Space Gear in Japan is known simply as the Mitsubishi L400, and is a well-respected commercial holdall. And yet, as with so many van designs these days, it has been cleverly and effectively transformed into an MPV by Mitsubishi. This MPV was then given the all-wheel-drive treatment and became a real off-roader. And no wonder, when you realise what lies beneath.

The Delica Space Gear is based on the chassis and running gear of the second-generation Pajero. It has the same powerplants and underpinnings; the same dual-range transfer box and transmission. In most cases, that results in a powerful and torquey 2.8-litre turbo diesel with intercooler, linked to an automatic gearbox (a Japanese favourite) and part-time twin-range four-wheel drive. This is an MPV like no other MPV; this one really will venture away from the tarmac and head for the hills.

Yet it's the sheer practicality of the Delica that still impresses most. Despite being no larger than an average family saloon, this all-wheel-drive people mover has an amazing amount of space on board. Access to the centre and rear seats is easy thanks to the single sliding door on the nearside; and with one third of the centre seat folded away, it's simplicity itself to clamber onto the back row. Unlike so many people carriers that have come and gone over the years, you don't need to be a professional contortionist in order to take your place as a passenger in a Delica Space Gear.

Like its equivalent Shogun/Pajero cousin, the Delica uses rear-wheel drive for normal on-road use, which obviously helps to reduce driveline drag and therefore improve fuel consumption. When the going gets tough, it's child's play to select high-ratio four-wheel drive, with low-ratio gearing on tap for more severe off-roading. All pretty standard stuff – but not for an MPV!

Any Delicas you see on Britain's roads (and there are a lot of them now) have been imported secondhand by specialists throughout the country. For a large proportion of used-4x4 buyers who put practicality high up their list of priorities, this particular Japanese 'grey' import is difficult not to justify. It's not for everyone, but it's an interesting addition to the Shogun/Pajero family, and many specialist importers just can't get enough of them.

The 1996 example shown in the photographs was

loaned to us by Midlands-based Car Choice Direct, a company that imports used Pajeros and Delicas from Japan, and the company's Andy Carter is a big fan of the Delica: 'There's no other MPV quite the same – how many off-roaders are this capable in the rough with this many people on board? Every Delica Space Gear we bring over gets sold incredibly quickly. It's getting to be a very popular import.'

It sounds as though Mitsubishi missed out on an opportunity for some extra British sales by deciding not to officially import new Delicas.

More Mitsubishis arrive...

However, Mitsubishi's niche-spotting abilities came to the fore once again soon after the initial expansion of the 21st century Shogun/Pajero range to three separate models, this time via the potential of 4x4 commercial vehicles. Suddenly, the highly respected L200 all-wheel-drive pick-up range was joined by van versions of the Shogun Pinin, Shogun Sport and even the Shogun itself, transforming Mitsubishi's commercial vehicle range from a single model to a complete and comprehensive line-up of 21 variations in an instant.

The new range was, logically enough, known as 4Work – a title that summed up its appeal rather neatly. Why should drivers of commercial vehicles not enjoy the same pleasures and off-road capabilities as those lucky enough to run top-quality SUVs? Why not indeed?

So much space, such easy access. The Delica Space Gear's combination of off-road capabilities and MPV-style practicalities has won the model many friends over the years. British buyers of 'grey' imports are particular fans. *(Author)*

Just when you thought the L200 truck was the only Mitsubishi commercial vehicle on sale in Europe, along comes this amazing line-up! Van versions of the Shogun, Shogun Pinin and Shogun Sport have filled an important niche in the market. *(Mitsubishi)*

The Shogun Pinin Van may not have the largest capacity in its class, but it's a useful little tool that also offers great value for money. As a compact delivery vehicle with genuine off-road abilities, it has been an interesting addition to the line-up. *(Mitsubishi)*

Is this the most stylish 4x4 van ever produced? Quite likely. The Shogun 4Work offered the same on- and off-road capabilities as its passenger-carrying cousins, but in a hard-working commercial package. A tempting choice. *(Mitsubishi)*

The market for all-wheel-drive commercial vehicles may not be vast, but it's a steady one – and it didn't cost Mitsubishi a fortune to enter, given that its new arrivals were all 'panelled-in' versions of existing 4x4s.

Remove the back seat, blank out the rear side windows and make sure there's a nice, flat load area – and that's it! Suddenly you have a hard-working, VAT-reclaimable van on your hands – and Mitsubishi has enjoyed much success with all its 4Work models.

Indeed, Mitsubishi now seems determined to make the most of every sector of the 4x4 scene, and the announcement of the new Outlander at the end of 2003 was proof of this.

Up until then, Mitsubishi had apparently never seen the need for a European-market all-wheel-drive 'crossover' estate, a potential rival to the all-conquering Subaru Forester. But then the Outlander arrived, itself based on the Japanese-market Airtrek, albeit with a complete interior and exterior redesign to give it extra appeal to European buyers. Mitsubishi found itself with yet another 4x4 market well and truly covered.

For fans of 'proper' 4x4s like the Shogun, Pajero and Challenger, the arrival of the Outlander was probably of little significance, but at least it proved that Mitsubishi was still intent on making the most of the world's thriving all-wheel-drive market, despite its own falling sales (particularly in Japan) and various financial disasters of the early 21st century putting the company's cashflow situation on the critical list.

But what does the future hold for the Shogun/Pajero brand itself? Rest assured, all the existing ranges will be replaced at some point in the future, assuming Mitsubishi has the financial clout to survive and prosper in the years ahead. The names of Shogun and Pajero are far too important – and far too valuable – not to be exploited still further. But exactly what the Shogun/Pajero of tomorrow will look like … only Mitsubishi knows the answer to that one.

Hyundai Galloper

Did you know the Series I Shogun/Pajero is still alive and well in downtown Korea? It's true. The major difference is that it's now known as the Hyundai Galloper. You may even have seen some examples on the road during your holidays in France, Germany and Spain – three of the main European markets where the Galloper has had a presence over the years.

The major difference between the Galloper and the early Shogun/Pajero is its modified front end, with a pair of slanted oblong headlamps in place of the

By launching the Outlander, Mitsubishi finally entered the 'crossover' estate market dominated by Subaru. It marked a useful addition to the company's 4x4 range and soon gained a niche following among fans of such vehicles. (Mitsubishi)

At first glance it looks like a short-wheelbase Series I Pajero. But no, this is the Korean-built Hyundai Galloper, a model never officially sold in the UK but fairly successful in certain key European markets. This example was spotted in Gran Canaria. *(Author)*

Shogun's round versions. This also gives the bonnet's leading edge a different shape, while the front grille is exclusive to the Hyundai. Some of the very latest versions for the Korean market even feature a rather bizarre-looking body kit – not something that would appeal to European tastes, I feel.

'Engineered by Mitsubishi', it says. That the Hyundai Galloper has enjoyed success for so many years after the demise of its Pajero equivalent is remarkable. *(Author)*

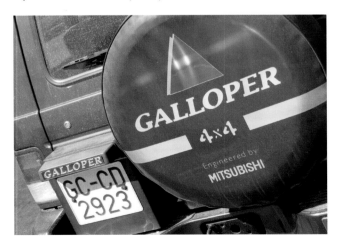

These days, only the short-wheelbase Galloper is produced, the long-wheelbase having effectively been replaced by more modern Hyundai 4x4s in recent years – including the Terracan and the Santa Fe. Despite the age of its basic design, it's remarkably faithful to the original Shogun/Pajero of 1982.

Engine options comprise 2.5-litre turbo-diesel (with or without intercooler) and 3.0-litre V6 petrol units, with a choice of manual or automatic transmission. The dual-range transfer box is complemented by a Mitsubishi-designed limited slip differential. In fact, just about everything under the Galloper's skin is pure Shogun/Pajero.

It's amazing, when you think about it, that the Galloper is still in production. Its design dates back well over two decades, after all, and could legitimately be termed a 'Mitsubishi cast-off'. That could be seen as almost embarrassing for the mighty Hyundai/Kia organisation, which by 2004 was officially the world's eighth largest motor manufacturer. Happily though, Hyundai doesn't seem bothered; and as long as there's demand for the Galloper, it will probably remain in production.

New-generation Hyundai 4x4s may be more sophisticated, more modern and more popular. But the Galloper's good, old-fashioned qualities ensure it still has many friends, even after all these years in production. Let's hope it continues to have them for a long time to come.

Chapter Five

The importance of imports

It's hard to think of another vehicle that has been more successful as an unofficial import than the Mitsubishi Pajero. In fact, for many years, the number of imports of used Pajeros from Japan has far outstripped sales of new Shoguns in the UK, and we're now in a situation where there are more 'unofficial' Pajeros on British roads than there are 'official' Shoguns.

Exactly why the Pajero has achieved such a cult following among fans of 'grey' imports is interesting. The prime reason, of course, is the sheer number of available used Pajeros in Japan, an indication of just how popular this model has been since the early 1980s.

But it's Mitsubishi's insistence on marketing Shogun and Pajero as upmarket brands that has also been responsible for the popularity of 'grey' imports. A desirable image has helped to keep residual values in the UK and throughout Europe surprisingly high over the years, which has made it well worthwhile for enterprising importers to bring shiploads of Pajeros over from their homeland. Even when purchase prices and the cost of shipping and import duty are taken into account, there's still enough of a profit margin to tempt many British dealers into going the 'grey' import route.

Of course, there are pitfalls for both trade and private importers to consider – and we'll come to some of those further on. But what exactly are the benefits for any potential owner who chooses a Pajero over a Shogun?

Exploding myths

Let's get one thing straight right now: a Pajero is not a cheaper vehicle to buy than its Shogun equivalent in the UK. Forget what you may have read in various motoring magazines in recent years, some of them claiming you could save at least £1000 by buying a used Pajero instead of an 'official' Shogun. It just isn't the case. In

fact, most of the time you'll find yourself paying out slightly MORE for a Pajero; but why is this?

Simply because you're getting more vehicle for your money. The Japanese have always liked their cars well

When it comes to Series II models, it's now more usual to see a 'grey' import Pajero on the streets of Britain than an 'official' Shogun. This superb 1999 Pajero five-door on sale with a specialist importer in 2004 is a typical example. *(Author)*

equipped, which is why most Pajeros that arrive from Japan are 'fully loaded'. It's unusual to find, say, a Series II Pajero without such niceties as electric windows all round, air conditioning, electrically adjustable door mirrors and much more – sometimes even leather upholstery. By comparison, an entry-level Shogun of the same vintage seems positively spartan.

Admittedly, not every Japanese-spec Pajero ever produced has been fantastically well equipped. But examples that have found themselves exported from The Land of the Rising Sun in later years have tended to be top-of-the-range versions such as the Exceed model – with its superior equipment, luxury and feel-good factor.

Britain and Ireland are unusual in Europe for being natural homes to secondhand Japanese imports, thanks to both countries driving on the left and using (primarily) right-hand-drive vehicles – just as in Japan. Consequently, more exports of used vehicles from Japan are sent to Britain than just about anywhere else. And the British, it seems, just can't get enough of them.

Japanese 'grey' imports aren't confined solely to Mitsubishi Pajeros, of course. Other 4x4s from Japan that have quite a following in the UK include the Isuzu Bighorn (Trooper), Nissan Terrano, Toyota Surf and the Pajero's cousin, the Mitsubishi Delica. But it's not just 4x4s that make popular imports; sports cars are almost as ubiquitous, with the Mazda Eunos (MX-5) in particular being seen as almost mainstream these days.

As the numbers of 'grey' imports have increased, so has their acceptability. In the mid-1990s, many so-called experts advised against buying any secondhand Japanese import because of uncertainty over spares availability, insurance hassles and the sheer complication of bringing the vehicles over in the first place. Happily though, such wariness is more or less a thing of the past, and many people who had previously shied away from owning a 'grey' import are now more than happy with their choice of a Pajero.

With greater acceptability these days, life with a 'grey' import has become much easier. Official Mitsubishi dealers are able to supply Pajero parts, as are the many independent spares and accessories specialists that can be found throughout the UK (see Appendix A for a list of some of the most popular).

As you'll read in Chapter Eight, even the issue of insurance is a lot less complicated than it used to be; yes, you'll end up paying more to insure a Japanese-spec Pajero than you would for an 'official' Shogun of the same age, but at least most insurers are now actually willing to offer cover. And that in itself is a major step forward. For more specific information on insurance, take a look at Chapter Eight.

Not so easy ...

As you might expect though, there are some pitfalls along the way for anybody who is new to the world of 'grey' imports, which is why this chapter offers plenty of good advice for all newcomers.

Obviously, the easiest way to buy a secondhand Pajero is to visit a specialist dealer who actually imports the vehicles from Japan and simply to choose the example you want. And there's no shortage of them; glance through any specialist magazine, such as *4x4 Mart*, *4x4* or *What 4x4 and MPV?* and you'll find adverts a-plenty for dealers offering just such a service. They bring Pajeros to the UK in small quantities at a time, deal with all the paperwork, sort out the necessary testing, pay any duties that are due and then sell the vehicles on to waiting British customers. From a consumer's point of view, it's as easy as buying any British-spec vehicle; all the hard work is done for you.

Perhaps you fancy a challenge, though? Maybe you like the idea of importing a secondhand Japanese vehicle yourself? Well, it is possible; but it's not necessarily easy, and you run the risk of hitting numerous snags and financial difficulties along the way. We'll cover the major pitfalls a little further on. Be under no illusion, though: becoming a 'do-it-yourself' importer in an effort to save yourself some cash is not something to be undertaken lightly.

Most of the 'grey' import Pajeros brought to the UK from Japan each year are top-of-the-range Exceed versions. British buyers now share the same love of luxury as the Japanese. *(Author)*

Dealing with the dealers

Assuming you want an easy time when buying a 'grey' import, you'll be making a sensible decision if you decide to buy direct from a specialist dealer who brings the vehicles over from Japan. In the main, such outfits know their stuff and they often have the best stock available on the open market. However, as with any industry, not every 'grey' importer is completely scrupulous or honest. One dealer I spoke with whilst researching this book admitted there are plenty of importers who consider it almost compulsory to 'clock' their Pajeros before putting them on sale.

One condition of making an ex-Japanese Pajero road-legal in the UK is to have its speed shown in miles-per-hour rather than kilometres-per-hour – but it's not compulsory to have the vehicle's 'mileage' shown in miles. That's why a lot of importers simply fit a conversion sticker over the speedometer to show the speed in mph, without then bothering to swap the odometer to a new one displaying miles.

Inevitably, it's easy enough to show a false 'mileage'. Anybody who is practical with a screwdriver can alter the original kilometres shown on the odometer to a drastically lower figure; or, if the importer is changing

The easiest and safest way to buy a 'grey' import is to head to a specialist dealer or importer and simply pick one from stock. There are plenty of importers around, most of which offer a good service and an excellent array of vehicles. *(Author)*

Can you be sure the 'grey' Pajero you're thinking of buying hasn't had its mileage altered since it arrived in the UK? Failure to carry out vital checks before you hand over the cash is foolhardy in the extreme. *(Author)*

If you're buying from a specialist importer, always make sure they're a member of BIMTA – and insist on a Certificate of Authenticity and odometer check before you buy. Check out BIMTA's website for further details. *(Author)*

the entire speedometer/odometer combination for a new one, he can easily make sure the 'new' miles are far fewer than they should be.

An importer I spoke to claimed Pajeros have even been known to have their mileages altered before they've left their ship at the British dockside: 'Clocking tends not to go on in Japan, as it's simply not part of their motoring scene,' he explained. 'But once the vehicles arrive in Britain, anything can happen before they get registered and passed on to their next owner. It's a real problem that every buyer should be aware of.'

Let me stress here that the vast majority of 'grey'

Thanks to the efforts of BIMTA, it is now possible to check how many kilometres just about any 'grey' import had covered by the time it left Japan. Most cars arriving from Japan have been sold via one of the major auction houses over there. *(Author)*

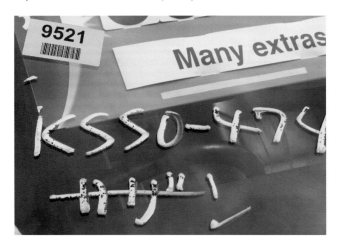

importers in the UK operate legal, honest and successful businesses, and have many satisfied customers to their credit. The importers with far fewer scruples are, thankfully, in the minority; but you still need to take every precaution to reduce the risks of buying a dud.

First of all, make sure the dealer you're buying from is a member of the British Independent Motor Trade Association (BIMTA), an established organisation that offers supporting services throughout the UK. In the event of any dispute between a member of the public and an importer, BIMTA can get involved and offer a conciliatory service – but only if the company concerned is a current member. All member dealers will be able to offer proof of their membership, so don't be afraid to ask to see this before you buy any recently imported Pajero. However, it's also wise to check their membership via BIMTA themselves if you're in any doubt.

BIMTA represents around 150 non-franchised British dealers, a large proportion of which are importers of Japanese vehicles. It has been in existence since 1997 and claims to be recognised by the Government as '...the voice of the independent sector'.

Indeed there's even more usefulness to BIMTA than you're probably expecting. Despite this being essentially a trade association, it can be of direct benefit to private buyers of imported vehicles, thanks to its Certificates of Authenticity and its odometer checks.

When buying from a BIMTA member, make sure you ask them to provide an official BIMTA Certificate of Authenticity specifically for the Pajero you're interested in. This doesn't cost the dealer a great deal, but it offers you invaluable peace of mind. Every year, BIMTA claims, around 2000 vehicles stolen in Japan end up being imported to the UK and sold on to unsuspecting buyers. But a BIMTA Certificate of Authenticity (which takes between five and ten working days to produce, on average) will confirm whether or not a vehicle was ever registered as stolen prior to being exported from Japan, and will also prove there's no outstanding finance on the vehicle. It's rather like an HPI check, but specifically for Japanese imports – and, thanks to BIMTA's unrivalled access to Japanese records, is simply unbeatable when it comes to the 'grey' import scene.

BIMTA can also provide odometer checks – and, again, this is a must if you're in any doubt about the vehicle you're buying or the dealer you're buying from. The vast majority of imports are sold in Japan via one of the country's 140 auction houses, and BIMTA has access to the records of almost all of them. This means an official odometer check can ascertain how many kilometres a vehicle had covered by the time it went under the hammer in Japan, making it easy for any buyer to prove whether or not it has since been 'clocked'. Again, the cost of this BIMTA service is low, which makes it a worthwhile exercise. And if the dealer you're hoping to buy from isn't willing to offer a BIMTA odometer check as part of the package, you've every right to be suspicious.

BIMTA is a trade association that's also extremely useful to Joe Public. For full details of how to contact them, see Appendix A. Ignore BIMTA at your peril!

Doing it yourself

Between 30,000 and 40,000 secondhand Japanese vehicles are imported to the UK each year, such is the demand for 'grey' imports. Almost invariably, there's a profit to be made, with most 'grey' importers reporting a steady increase in business from the late 1990s onwards. It's a growing scene, it seems.

But what if you want to bypass the dealer completely in an effort to save money? Is it possible to privately import a used car from Japan and cut out the dealer's profit margin? Well, yes, anything is possible, and many Brits manage to do this each year. Just as many though, end up losing significant sums of money, such are the many pitfalls along the way.

I'm not going into intricate detail here about every single step of the way and how to tackle the whole issue of private imports, mainly because I'm not advocating it as a realistic option for most people. But if you are intent on planning your own 'grey' import, there are certain important points you must be aware of.

For a start, it's essential that you have a reliable and dependable agent in Japan. Buying a car over there isn't simply a case of catching a plane, heading for the nearest Japanese car auction on your arrival, and waving your hand in the air until you come away with the Pajero of your dreams. Most car auctions in Japan are 'trade only', which means a British or European tourist would stand little chance of gaining access. Then there's the issue of what to do with the vehicle once the hammer falls and it's yours.

An agent in Japan should be able to arrange almost everything for you, from attending the auction and bidding on your behalf to such complicated issues as arranging transport to the docks, all the necessary paperwork, the actual shipping process and what

It's possible to import a vehicle from Japan yourself – but do the many risks and pitfalls really make it worthwhile? Do you understand all the procedures involved? It's a complicated business at the best of times. *(Author)*

happens once your vehicle arrives either in Southampton or Bristol. A good agent is worth every yen of his commission! However, before you give an agent the go-ahead, make sure you've seen some verifiable references from previous satisfied clients; if he's unable to supply these, don't take the risk.

The arrival of your Pajero in the UK marks the start of another complex process, as you must pay the import duty and VAT that is now due. HM Customs & Excise will insist the purchase price of the vehicle in Japan is liable for VAT, as is the cost of the import duties that must also be added. As one importer told me, 'You're

Most 'grey' imports arrive in the UK at either Southampton or Bristol – and that's the start of a potentially complex process of duties to be paid and tests to be passed. Don't underestimate the number of things that can (and probably will) go wrong. *(Author)*

Most Pajeros on British roads still have their nearside reversing mirrors fitted on the front wing – a mandatory part of the equipment list in Japan. *(Author)*

the suitability of a vehicle's instrumentation for British usage. Within ESVA is the requirement for a 'model report', applicable to most Japanese imports manufactured from January 1st 1997 onwards. The model report is a tool developed and produced by the Vehicle and Operator Services Agency (VOSA) from information supplied to them by official test centres. Their examiners then use the information on the model report to satisfy themselves that the vehicle being presented for ESVA testing is the same as a model originally tested.

And just because your vehicle has passed an ESVA test, don't assume it's automatically legal to use on the road once it's registered. ESVA is not a test of roadworthiness, so – assuming your Pajero is at least three years old – it will still need to pass a standard MoT test, too.

Is it a fair system? Well, it's not an easy one, that's for sure. And anybody hoping to import a vehicle for which a model report is not already available will have a major difficulty on their hands – not to mention the prospect of serious extra expense.

The cost of getting a Japanese import through an ESVA test varies hugely from model to model. However, most importers I spoke to reckoned on spending anywhere between £700 and £1500 (in 2004) per vehicle simply to meet ESVA criteria, before they could even think about trying to register the vehicles in the UK.

Import auctions

The risks and complications involved in finding yourself a reliable agent in Japan, who is able to source an import for you, can be avoided if you choose to attend one of several auction houses now specialising in freshly imported vehicles. One of the most popular is Motor Way auctions, ideally located in Southampton – but there are others, as a glance at Appendix A will confirm. So what happens at such auctions?

It's very much the same as an ordinary car auction, apart from the fact that all the vehicles being sold are freshly arrived in the UK and have yet to undergo ESVA testing or the registration process. It's a way of locating a vehicle that you can actually see before you buy, without having to pay any kind of a dealer's premium. However, as with importing a vehicle yourself, you then have to go through the ESVA (if applicable), MoT and registration processes before you can use the vehicle in the UK.

If that idea appeals, there are some good buys to be had, but if buying a secondhand Pajero needs to be as

paying tax on a tax – but there's nothing you can do about it.' You will be unable to bring your car away from the UK docks without first paying all the duty and tax that is due; and even then you won't be able to drive your Pajero home, as it still won't be registered for use on British roads.

Registration itself is relatively straightforward if the vehicle is at least ten years of age. Armed with all the paperwork for your newly-acquired Pajero, you should be able to arrange UK registration fairly easily via your nearest Vehicle Registration Office. If your Pajero is under ten years old though, this is where things get much more complicated.

Any Japanese import less than a decade old must now undergo an ESVA test (replacement for the original SVA test), introduced in 2004. Whereas the old SVA was simply a check to ensure any vehicle that was not 'type approved' for UK use was up to British and European standards, the ESVA is rather more stringent.

Extra criteria are covered within ESVA, including emissions, noise testing, fitment of suitable alarms and hassle-free as possible for you, there's still little substitute for buying your next Mitsubishi from a BIMTA-affiliated specialist dealer. It may not be the cheapest option, but it's certainly the least risky.

Condition is everything

The best news of all about buying a 'grey' import from any source is that the Japanese generally look after their vehicles extremely well. Anybody who has ever studied Japanese society will know that this is a very ordered and structured country with high levels of discipline – and this seems to filter its way through every aspect of Japanese life.

Not only are secondhand Pajeros in Japan generally in excellent condition, they also tend to have covered fewer miles (or rather, kilometres) than British-spec Shoguns. And because the Japanese climate is somewhat milder than the average British one, the vehicles also suffer less from the ravages of rust, as mentioned in Chapter Eight.

If a recently imported Pajero is showing any signs of wear and tear (scratched or grazed paintwork, for example), it will most probably have occurred since it was sold at auction in Japan. Once the hammer falls, any bound-for-Britain Pajero then has a lengthy and difficult journey ahead of it, being shunted from auction house to car park to ship to docks to car park over a period of several weeks. It's not unusual for parking damage to occur, and you need to be on the lookout for this (or for hastily carried out repair work) when inspecting any future purchase.

There are a few other things to remember too, when buying an ex-Japanese Pajero – no matter where the vehicle is being bought from. First, take a look at what kind of rust-proofing has been carried out; Japanese-spec Pajeros tend to be less well protected against corrosive road salt than their British-spec counterparts, and it may well be worth investing a little in a thorough, professional treatment of the underside with Waxoyl or similar. You will probably be able to negotiate this into the price if you're buying from a dealer, but always ensure the job has been done well and to your satisfaction.

Also, do check your Pajero's radio is working properly in the UK. A band expander usually needs to be fitted to enable you to receive British radio stations. It's neither an expensive nor a difficult job, but it's something you should expect any supplying dealer to have already sorted out for you.

Finally (although this is less relevant for potential

If a recently imported Pajero is showing signs of scratches or grazes to its paintwork, it probably happened during its lengthy journey from the Japanese auction house to the British dealer's forecourt. Insist on it being put right before you buy. *(Author)*

If you're buying a 'grey' Pajero, check that the radio works as it should. A band expander usually needs to be fitted before you can receive British radio stations. It's not an expensive job, but an important one. *(Author)*

There are so many Pajeros on British roads now, it's easy enough to buy one privately that has already been in the UK for some time. Few imports have proved as popular as the Pajero over the years. *(Richard Aucock)*

Pajero owners than it is for fanatics of Japanese sports cars), did you know that every vehicle sold in Japan has an artificially limited top speed of just 180km/h (112.5mph)? It won't worry the owner of an old turbo-diesel Pajero, for obvious reasons; but it's a point worth mentioning.

The best advice?

So, if a 'grey' import Pajero is top of your list of requirements, how will you go about buying the best example you can afford – and from which source? Before you take the plunge, do some research of your own. Is there a specialist dealer in your area able to supply you with a 'grey' Pajero? Are they members of BIMTA? Are they willing to offer mileage and history guarantees, via BIMTA? Has the vehicle been through an SVA or ESVA test prior to being registered? Have you

looked into how much your insurance cover is going to cost? Do your homework, take your time, and always be prepared to shop around.

Of course, another alternative is to buy a Pajero privately, one that has already been in the UK for a while and is being sold by its current British owner. But pay particular attention to the claimed 'mileage' (is it in miles or kilometres? Is the figure guaranteed by the vendor?); and try to ascertain as much about the vehicle's previous history as you possibly can. If you've any doubts, walk away and find another used Pajero; there are plenty available.

In fact, by 2005, an estimated quarter of a million 'grey' imports of all kinds were registered in Britain, with the Pajero being amongst the most popular models. Nowadays it's easier to locate a Series II Pajero for sale in the UK than it is a Series II Shogun, such is the popularity of the model. Use this to your advantage, making sure you buy the very best example your budget will allow. Get it right and there's no reason why life with a 'grey' import shouldn't be a positive experience.

Choosing your Shogun/Pajero

It will come as no surprise to learn that your most suitable choice of Shogun or Pajero will depend largely upon your budget. As with any vehicle launched more than twenty years ago that's still in production, values of used Shoguns and Pajeros vary enormously. And so do their various specifications – which means it's not simply a case of opting for the first example you come across that falls within your price range.

It's important to weigh up your own requirements and what you expect from a Shogun or Pajero, particularly if you're the first-time buyer of a 4x4. Indeed, it's astonishing just how many people running Shoguns and Pajeros these days report that they've never owned a 4x4 of any kind before. So what was it that swayed them in the direction of the finest Mitsubishi product?

Towing the line

As I talked with various importers of used Pajeros during research for this book, they confirmed to me that a large proportion of their buyers need a top-notch

The Shogun/Pajero is a particularly popular buy among people who have never owned a 4x4 before. They tend to be attracted by its reliability and, increasingly, its towing capabilities. But what do YOU need from your 4x4? *(Mitsubishi)*

All three generations of Shogun/Pajero have probably won more towing awards than any other 4x4 ever produced. The Series III, for example, was the Caravan Club's 'All Terrain' class winner in the Tow Car of the Year 2001 award. *(Mitsubishi)*

towing vehicle first and foremost; and it is people like this who have been responsible for a major shift in sales of used 4x4s over the last few years.

It wasn't very long ago that anybody with a caravan, a boat or a large trailer to haul around would simply buy a big-enough saloon or estate with sufficient power to do just that. But the 1990s saw increasing numbers of caravan owners in particular realising the benefits of running a full-size 4x4. With a caravan, after all, it's not just the actual towing process that's involved: there are also the family's belongings to stow away somewhere on board, as well as the kids, the dog and all manner of paraphernalia that are suddenly deemed essential for a fortnight's break in Cornwall or a spot of touring in the south of France. It's a similar story with anybody who tows a boat behind them, for the towing vehicle itself invariably becomes the general holdall for the vast amounts of equipment and supplies that are needed for a day on the water.

That's why most Shoguns and Pajeros that you see used as towing vehicles are the five-door, long-

wheelbase versions – irrespective of which generation of Mitsubishi we're talking about. Whatever the age of your five-door Shogun, you'll find it a great five-seater with a copious amount of luggage space in the back when the rearmost seats are folded away. But it is once the caravan or trailer is finally hitched behind that any Shogun/Pajero really comes into its own.

If caravan holidays were always hot and dry, there'd be no real need for all-wheel drive. But as anybody who has been caravanning will testify, the usefulness of all-wheel traction when trying to drag your home-from-home through a muddy caravan site can be priceless. Even with standard road tyres fitted (as is the case with most family-owned Shoguns and Pajeros), it shouldn't be too difficult to remove a caravan from even the trickiest mud bath.

It's not just the four-wheel drive aspect of the Shogun/Pajero that makes it a great towing vehicle, though. There's also – in the case of the turbo-diesel versions at least – the impressive levels of torque on offer. Even a basic 2477cc turbo-diesel Series II Shogun/Pajero from 1991–94 managed a healthy 177lb ft of torque, despite a fairly mediocre power output of 105bhp. As we learned in Chapter Two, those figures were seriously boosted in 1994 when the 2.8-litre version was introduced, resulting in a very impressive 215lb ft of torque at a mere 2000rpm. And it is these 2.8-litre Series II Shoguns that are still revered by so many owners as among the finest towing vehicles sensible money can buy. When it comes to towing, there's an argument that low-down torque is far more important than outright power – rather like when off-roading. Lots of torque when you're dragging a large caravan behind you makes for a more effortless driving experience: fewer gear changes, less strain on the engine and fewer problems when encountering steep hills or steady motorway inclines. The lower down the rev range the maximum torque is developed, the better it is in terms of usefulness; so, it would seem, a 2.8 turbo-diesel Shogun or Pajero has just the right combination for the job.

It also boasts some of the heftiest maximum towing weights you're likely to come across with any realistically priced, secondhand 4x4. In fact, even an old Series I 2.5-litre Shogun/Pajero is capable of hauling a seriously heavy load behind it – up to 3969lb, in fact, in the case of a braked trailer on pre-1987 models. After 1987, as mentioned in Chapter One, this was increased

to a claimed 7275lb, far more than most owners would ever require.

Just as having high torque levels helps to reduce engine strain and driver frustrations, towing a trailer or caravan that's well within the maximum allowed for your vehicle will help to keep your Shogun/Pajero in good shape. What's the point of buying a vehicle whose maximum towing weight only just exceeds the weight of your trailer or caravan, when you can spend the same money on a Shogun or Pajero that will do it with ease?

A few words of warning before you buy your Shogun or Pajero, however: the issue of maximum towing weights isn't simply a case of quoting what's claimed by the manufacturer. In the UK in particular, the law is a little more complicated than that – and it falls on you, the driver, to make sure your vehicle and trailer/caravan combination is legal and acceptable.

First of all, you'll need to know your caravan's

Most UK-spec Shoguns already have towing brackets fitted as standard, but many 'grey' import Pajeros do not. Bear this in mind when haggling over price. *(Richard Aucock)*

COMPETITION WINNERS

If anybody ever suggests to you that your Shogun or Pajero isn't a proper off-roader, just mention the words 'Paris' and 'Dakar' to them. That should wipe the smug smile off their face...

Throughout the life of all incarnations of the Shogun/Pajero, this vehicle has proved itself time after time in one of the world's toughest, most gruelling challenges: the Paris-Dakar Rally, an 11,000-kilometre dash through some of the roughest terrain in no less than seven countries. It's one of the ultimate tests of a vehicle's strength, reliability and cross-country prowess – and it's one in which the specially prepared

No other company has enjoyed greater success in the Paris-Dakar than Mitsubishi. Shown here is the rally-winning Pajero in the 2001 event. *(Mitsubishi)*

Shogun/Pajero Evolution models have truly excelled over the years.

Since 1983, Mitsubishi has won the Paris-Dakar outright on no fewer than nine occasions – but the record-breaking doesn't end there. At the time of writing, the company has won the same event for four consecutive years (2001–2004), which is more than any rival. And it has also achieved a total of seven years when Pajeros have taken the top two places – 1992, 1997, 1998, 2001, 2002, 2003 and 2004. There isn't a manufacturer anywhere in the world that can match that kind of Paris-Dakar success.

Admittedly, the Pajeros used for the event are very different from the Shogun or Pajero you might have parked outside your front door. But the ancestry is there, and all the engineering involved is pure Mitsubishi. This is a company that knows more than most about reliability, durability and how to create a winning formula.

The Pajero Evolution that won the 2004 Paris-Dakar was the most impressive yet, thanks to its specially developed 4.0-litre 24-valve V6 engine, six-speed sequential gearchange and hugely upgraded full-time all-wheel-drive system with self-locking front and rear differentials and automatically locking centre diff. The independent suspension set-up too, was textbook stuff thanks to a pair of Donerre shock absorbers per wheel, fully adjustable damping, double wishbones and coil springs all round. Finishing the basic specification for this long-haul rally-winning machine was the essential 500-litre fuel tank – a tad larger than you get with your average caravan-towing Shogun...

With the Pajero Evolution's success in Paris-Dakar, and the Lancer WRC04's competitiveness throughout the World Rally Championship, Mitsubishi's involvement in motor sport was healthier than ever by 2004; and that can only be good news. If nothing else, it reinforces the public's perception that Mitsubishi really knows about off-road challenges. As far as production vehicle sales are concerned, that can do no harm at all.

Competition success has had a more direct influence on the Shogun/Pajero than you might expect. Pajero Evolution models, inspired by the Paris-Dakar winners, have been sold in Japan and certain key export markets over the years, offering class-beating performance by SUV standards. Admittedly, they were positively tame compared with the specially developed Evolutions that took Paris-Dakar by storm; but as a more powerful and significantly quicker version of Mitsubishi's ever-popular 4x4, the Series II Pajero Evolution, in particular, gained something of a following.

At least the older winning Pajeros looked like Pajeros. This monstrous victor from 2004 bore little resemblance to any Shogun/Pajero we'd ever seen on the roads! (*Mitsubishi*)

Does the towing bracket on your Shogun or Pajero come with official type approval? If it has been fitted since 1998, it should. Check it out to make sure. *(Author)*

'maximum technically permissible laden mass' (MTPLM) if it was built in 1998 or later; if it's a pre-1998 caravan, you'll need to find out its 'maximum gross weight' (MGW). You then need to know the kerb weight, nose weight and maximum towing limit for the specific Shogun or Pajero you intend to use for towing – and it has to be the exact model, as these do vary depending on wheelbase, engine choice and so on. You then need to ensure that your caravan's MTPLM does not exceed 85 per cent of your car's kerb weight; to do this, divide the actual laden weight of your caravan by the kerb weight of the towing vehicle, and then multiply by 100.

The closer the resultant figure gets to 85 per cent, the more difficult will towing become, which is why it is recommended to buy a vehicle capable of towing far more than you intend, as it will make for a safer and more pleasant towing experience all round.

If all this is starting to sound rather complicated, don't worry. There's an organisation in the UK that will work out everything for you, based upon the make, model and year of both your towing vehicle and your caravan. Thanks to their unrivalled database of weights and specifications, they will be able to tell you almost immediately whether the Shogun and caravan combination you're intending to purchase will be both safe and legal. See Appendix A for the contact details of Towsafe – and make sure you don't take any chances.

In most European countries these days, and particularly in the UK, illegal towing is taken very seriously. If a car/caravan outfit is incorrectly matched, British motorists can be looking at a fine of up to £1000

and three penalty points on their driving licence; taking any kind of a towing risk is both dangerous and illegal.

No wonder today's secondhand Shoguns and Pajeros are seen as such sensible choices for buyers who need to tow. With such promising maximum towing weights quoted by Mitsubishi, it would be difficult for most owners to haul around more than the capacity of their vehicle. Even so, it pays not to take any chances; in the UK, confirmation may be obtained from Towsafe (who will provide up to five checks for different combinations for a very reasonable registration fee), and is surely money well spent.

One final point about towing, and it's all to do with your vehicle's actual towing bracket. In Britain, only towing brackets with official type approval should have been fitted since August 1st, 1998. Bear this in mind when buying a bracket – or, indeed, when buying any vehicle already fitted with a towing bracket. Are you completely confident your towing bracket is both safe and legal? If in any doubt, have a modern replacement professionally fitted without delay.

Head for the hills

If a long-wheelbase diesel-powered Shogun/Pajero is the vehicle of choice for towing (thanks to its spaciousness, its generous maximum permissible towing weights and its high torque levels), what's recommended for those buyers who don't need to tow but who do need to venture regularly off-road?

The logical answer would be: a short-wheelbase model. Serious off-roaders, almost irrespective of the make and model they favour, tend to opt for the smaller versions available. Whether it's a Land Rover, an Isuzu Trooper or a Suzuki Vitara that's being bought for mud-plugging, it's usually the short-wheelbase derivative that's seen as the most desirable for rough-stuff action. The reason for that is both obvious and logical: with less distance between the front and rear axles, there's less chance of getting 'grounded' on the apex of a hill or when traversing a series of deep ruts and ridges.

Not everybody has always been complimentary about the off-road capabilities of even the short-wheelbase Shogun/Pajero. Motoring author Jack Jackson, writing in his 1988 reprint of *The Off-Road Four-Wheel Drive Book*, commented: 'Despite the claimed 8.3-inch ground clearance, it gets bogged down as soon as it looks at soft sand or deep mud. On paper the Pajero has more ground clearance than a Range Rover, but it has much more underneath to catch, and poor rear overhang on the long-wheelbase. It is soon bogged

Above: Not everyone has always had good things to say about the Shogun/Pajero's off-road prowess, although perhaps they should remember to compare like with like? A Pajero has never pretended to be a Land Rover Defender, after all. *(Mitsubishi)*

Below: Just about any Shogun or Pajero will go off-road quite successfully. But the enormous rear overhang on this Series III five-door could be a problem when tackling a steep uphill gradient. *(Mitsubishi)*

down if it tries to follow the ruts made by Land Rovers or Range Rovers…'

How fair are such comments? It depends on what your off-road priorities are, in my opinion. I'll be the first to admit that if your reason for buying a secondhand 4x4 is purely to enjoy 4x4 fun days or even to take part in off-road competitions, the Shogun/Pajero isn't the most obvious choice. This, after all, is a vehicle designed from the outset as a civilised 4x4 rather than an out and out off-roader capable of beating Land Rovers at their own game. As he's an avid off-road fanatic, Jack Jackson's priorities are probably different from those of most potential Shogun/Pajero buyers, and his criticisms, presumably, stem from this.

Anybody in the market for an affordable off-road machine intended for weekend fun in the rough tends to steer towards elderly Land Rovers and – increasingly – Suzuki SJs. Both models, although very different in size and character, are the favourites of those in the off-

road fraternity who do things on a fairly tight budget. Both vehicles offer good ground clearance, terrific traction, simple engineering and, above all else, a wide range of readily available modifications for making them even more competent in extreme off-road situations. No wonder good examples are usually snapped up as soon as they become available, given the increasing interest these days in the off-road scene.

But the Shogun/Pajero doesn't fall into that category. Yes, you do see them heading off-road; indeed, I've been to countless off-road fun days over the years where there's usually been at least one Shogun or Pajero taking part, its owner keen to find out just what the vehicle is capable of away from the tarmac. But if a 4x4 is being bought purely and simply for fun in ultra-tough terrain, it's rare for a Shogun/Pajero to be top of the wanted list. This doesn't mean that the Mitsubishi isn't capable of fulfilling most owners' off-road needs. When it comes to green laning, traversing unmade farm tracks, tackling steep inclines and the like, any Shogun or Pajero will be more than capable – and even more so if a set of off-road tyres is fitted in place of the standard rubber. If your off-road needs go further than this,

A Shogun/Pajero's standard ground clearance is adequate for most owners' needs, but remember that add-ons such as the side steps fitted here can hamper off-road progress. *(Richard Aucock)*

there's quite a lot that can be done to make the Shogun/Pajero a more competent machine in the rough, as we'll see in Chapter Nine.

Assuming your off-road requirements aren't in the same league as those of the owner of a highly modified Land Rover who enters 4x4 competitions every weekend, there's every chance you'll be more than satisfied with the capabilities of your Mitsubishi. After all, it has all the right ingredients – from the dual-range transfer box fitted to all variants to the generously high torque levels of the diesel models. And it is the turbo-diesel Shoguns and Pajeros that, as with most other 4x4s, seem to make the most sense off-road, thanks to the extra torque as well as their greater fuel economy when tackling tough terrain in low-ratio all-wheel drive.

The question of ground clearance is an essential one when discussing off-roading, as we've already seen. But although the Shogun/Pajero's clearance may not be in the same class as that of many Land Rovers and Range Rovers, it's certainly adequate for most uses. In any case, as we'll see further on in the book, there are a few tricks available to any owner wishing to increase the vehicle's ride height and ground clearance.

The subject of front and rear overhangs is also of concern to 'real' off-roaders, and again it's the short-wheelbase Shogun/Pajero that wins hands down here, lacking the longer rear overhang of the five-door Series I and II models. Always remember too, that a towing bracket fitted to your Shogun or Pajero can cause problems when off-roading, as it tends to get caught in the mud as you begin your climb of a particularly steep slope; the electrics of your towing bracket can also get damaged by water and mud when off-roading, so it pays to check these regularly to ensure they're working as they should.

Tough choices

Whichever model of Shogun or Pajero you end up with parked on your driveway, you can be sure you've invested your money in one of the most durable, most reliable, most capable 4x4s that money can buy. This is

When it comes to choosing a tough and reliable machine that will thrive on hard work for as long as you need it to, there's little to touch a Series II Shogun/Pajero. This 3.0-litre V6 requires less servicing than a turbo diesel. (*Author*)

particularly true, again, in Series I and II guises, with all versions doing exactly what their owners expect of them. When it comes to ultimate reliability, both the petrol and diesel engines are broadly similar in longevity, but remember that a diesel will require far more regular servicing – and this may be a consideration if your annual mileage is fairly high. On the other hand, the extra fuel economy of a diesel Shogun/Pajero should more than make up for the added maintenance costs.

So your final choice of model will depend very much on your own priorities and requirements. For example, if you don't have a large family and you rarely need to carry five people and their luggage in your vehicle, do you really need a long-wheelbase Shogun or Pajero? A three-door short-wheelbase model will be cheaper to buy, more frugal on fuel, more manoeuvrable and easier to park. It may not have quite the same 'presence' as a long-wheelbase version, but is image alone really worth the extra expense and inconvenience involved?

On the other hand, don't underestimate your family's needs. Just because a short-wheelbase Shogun you've seen advertised seems remarkably good value, don't jump in and snap it up without first evaluating whether you can really manage with a three-door vehicle and whether it's really going to be large enough for your needs. Two months down the line you could realise you need a bigger 4x4 and your short-wheelbase model could be back on the market.

Automatic option?

A quick word here about prejudice – particularly when it comes to automatic transmission. British buyers have traditionally been very different from American and Japanese motorists in their attitudes towards autos. Find an American driver who really knows what to do with a 'stick shift' (that's American-speak for a manual gearchange) and you've got a rare commodity on your hands; the British, though, tend to view automatic gearboxes with suspicion. But why?

In my experience, any Shogun or Pajero fitted with automatic transmission tends to be a more relaxing drive – and potentially more reliable, too. After all, we're not talking performance machines here, so any minor loss of acceleration involved with automatic

Above: Any automatic Shogun/Pajero should offer smooth gear changes and a much more relaxing driving style. The auto gearboxes themselves tend to be reliable, even over vast mileages. *(Author)*

transmission is hardly relevant when it comes to a large 4x4. You also won't have a replacement clutch to worry about at a later date (which can be a problem with any 4x4 that endures regular off-road use or spends much of its time towing a heavy load), while the auto gearboxes used throughout the Shogun's career have been reliable, long-lasting units. Automatic transmission just seems to suit the big Mitsubishi so perfectly, and it's a mystery to me why anybody would deliberately opt for a manual model.

But people do, which means they're also missing out on a huge proportion of the imported Pajeros that have found themselves brought over from Japan. The Japanese rarely opt for manual transmission with a Pajero, which obviously limits the choice of any Brit who won't drive anything else. So my advice is to try a Shogun or Pajero with automatic transmission before you dismiss it out of hand; you never know, you might become a convert!

Whichever size, model or age of Shogun or Pajero you end up with, be satisfied with one thing: you've made an excellent choice. Get one in the very best condition your budget will allow and you're in with a decent chance of enjoying many thousands of miles of happy, trouble-free 4x4ing. The following chapter will help you to make the right choice.

Left: Most 'grey' imports come with automatic transmission, such is the Japanese buyer's love of autos. If you're adamant you prefer manual to automatic, take a long test drive before you finally make up your mind. You might just be converted! *(Author)*

Taking the plunge

You've made your decision about which Mitsubishi Shogun or Pajero you want. Or, perhaps, simply which you can afford. Now it's time to get out there and start checking out examples for sale. Before you do that, though, you need to know what you're looking for, what might go wrong and how you can best avoid getting ripped-off.

Whether buying privately or from a dealer, take your time and don't be afraid to check out any claims made by the vendor. It's at this stage that your head needs to rule your heart. *(Richard Aucock)*

Before we get on to the specifics, I'll just offer a few words of caution about buying used cars in general. At the best of times, it's a minefield of dangers and pitfalls; and when you see a Shogun/Pajero that seems to be exactly the one you've been searching high and low for, it's so easy to get carried away in the excitement and forget some basic procedures. That's when you're particularly vulnerable.

So, for a start, when buying any used vehicle, only ever arrange to meet the vendor at their own home or (in the case of a dealer) at their premises. Meeting

'halfway' or arranging to have the car brought to your address is a classic ploy used by vendors who don't actually own the vehicles in question.

When you get to the vendor's house, ask to see the vehicle's V5 or V5C (in the UK) registration document and check that the vendor's name and the address shown on the V5/V5C correspond with where you actually are. If you've any doubts or concerns, simply walk away. And if there's no V5 or V5C offered with the vehicle at all (I haven't long moved house and the log book's still at the DVLA, the vendor may claim), don't buy the vehicle under any circumstances, no matter how tempting it seems.

Checking the genuineness of a vehicle goes much further, though. Still with the V5/V5C in your hand, take a look at the Mitsubishi's VIN number; check it with the number that's printed on the V5/V5C and, if there's any discrepancy whatsoever, don't even consider buying the car. It's that simple.

At this stage, and assuming you're examining a UK-spec Shogun rather than an imported Pajero (which I'll deal with a little further on), you also need to be looking into the car's service history, to check that what the vendor claims to be a full service history actually is, as well as using this to help verify the mileage. Never accept it if a vendor claims …the service book is still at the garage; I forgot to pick it up when I had the car serviced last week. If a service history is boasted about, you want to be able to see it in front of you before you even consider making an offer.

Don't be afraid to spend time carefully studying the service book and any previous MoT certificates that are with the car, too. Check that all the mileages shown on certain dates seem to tally with what's being claimed about the vehicle. You might even want to make a note of the previous owner's name and address, approaching them before you hand over any money to ensure they can back up what you've been told and vouch for the car's history.

Another obvious point when viewing any used car is to look for signs of a forced entry, which relates to the previous point about checking out the vendor's actual ownership. It's a sad fact of life that many thousands of cars get broken into each year, so any signs of a previous break-in may simply have occurred during the current keeper's ownership; don't be afraid to ask, because there's no reason why they should hide this from you. If, however, you can clearly see that a door lock has been forced, the steering column shroud looks strangely loose or you can see signs of shattered

Is that a genuine mileage? Can the vendor guarantee it? Is there any evidence to support it? Make sure you check carefully any service history and previous MoTs that come with the vehicle. *(Author)*

glass inside the car, you've every right to have your suspicions aroused when the vendor denies all knowledge.

You also need to be on the lookout for signs of previous accident damage – some of which, in the case of an imported Pajero, could have happened relatively

Not all signs of previous accident damage will be this obvious! Check for patches of dull paintwork, over-spray, ripples in the paint or signs of body filler beneath. A vendor's claim of an accident-free record may not be true. *(Author)*

Above: Check thoroughly for obvious signs of fresh paintwork or poor quality repairs. Don't be afraid to open all the doors and look carefully around the edges and along the sills for 'join' lines or an overlap in the paint. *(Author)*

Left: Be realistic in your expectations. A cheap and cheerful Series I Pajero probably won't be in pristine condition, but it should be structurally sound if you're to avoid major expense when the next MoT test is due. *(Author)*

recently whilst being shipped from Japan. Particularly on younger vehicles, check for mismatched paintwork (colour, finish and so on); ripples in body panels (possible evidence of body filler or poor repair work); signs of over-spray; wheels that seem out of alignment; obvious replacement of inner panel work under the bonnet. The list goes on, but just a couple of these points should be enough to make you suspicious and question the vendor's claiming …she's never been in an accident.

How thoroughly you follow this kind of advice will depend partly on how much you're paying for your Shogun or Pajero, how old it is and what you're intending to use it for. Let's face it, checking for panel damage on a 20-year-old Series I that's going to be used solely as a working tool is not going to be as important to you as it would be for the buyer of a 12-month-old Shogun Warrior. Be realistic in your approach, but always be on the lookout for vendors' stories that just don't add up.

One final point worth mentioning before we move on to the specifics of various Shoguns and Pajeros is this: professional car inspections. You can pay for an expert to come along and thoroughly examine the vehicle you're thinking of buying. In the UK, the AA and RAC carry out such inspections, as do many private companies. Obviously, when it comes to an old, low-value Shogun with a fortnight's MoT left to run, it's not an economically viable proposition; on such a vehicle, you can't exactly expect perfection, but I'd advise anybody thinking of buying a more expensive used car to consider paying for an independent inspection. If they find any minor faults you might have missed, you'll be able to use this to negotiate the price downwards; and if they discover something major that makes you think twice about buying the car, surely that's also money well spent?

Such examinations usually include an HPI (a vehicle history checking service provided in the UK by HPI, the AA or the RAC) to ensure the car in question has never been registered as stolen or previously written off in an accident. This is essential information, and it's available to anybody with a phone and a credit card to pay for it. Even if you decide against a full independent inspection of a used vehicle, failure to have an HPI check carried out is arguably very foolish indeed.

Import issues

Some – but by no means all – of what you've already read in this chapter won't necessarily apply if it's an unofficially imported Pajero you're thinking of buying, one that's found its way over from Japan in recent years. Obviously, you still need to carry out the same checks for accident damage, signs of abuse, VIN number matching and so on; that's logical enough. But such issues as service history and previous MoTs aren't quite so straightforward.

There's still a good trade in secondhand Pajero imports, with Series IIs in particular being shipped to the UK in fairly hefty numbers each year. Indeed, there are now more Japanese-spec Pajeros on the roads of Britain than there are British-spec Shoguns. When you bear in mind that more than 75,000 Shoguns have been officially sold in the UK by Mitsubishi since 1983, it gives you an idea of the scale we're talking about here.

One specialist importer of used Pajeros I spoke to whilst writing this book was honest about the fact that he can't always guarantee the mileages of his vehicles.

The most common 'grey' import from the Pajero family is the Series II, a vehicle for which demand in the UK is still impressively high. No other 4x4 attracts quite such a fanatical following as a secondhand import. *(Richard Aucock)*

However, 'clocking' (the winding back of a car's mileage) is far less of a problem in Japan than it is in the UK, which means that – as he's a decent trader with a good reputation – there's every chance that the vehicles on his forecourt have never been tampered with in that way. Nevertheless, not every used car dealer in the UK is as honest as he is, and by the time a Pajero has found itself being bought and sold again a few times there's no guarantee that its mileage is genuine. So, it seems, the onus is on the prospective purchaser to verify as much as possible.

The main problem is that a lot of Japanese imports don't come with a service history – and those that do are obviously written in Japanese, which makes deciphering them something of a challenge. It also means that all the other paperwork that might come with the vehicle (handbooks, old receipts and so on) will also be in Japanese. Still, even a virtually

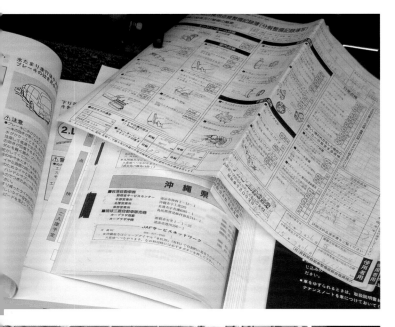

Even if your 'grey' import comes with a full service history, almost all of it will be in Japanese. Mind you, any service history is better than none at all... *(Author)*

unreadable service history is better than none, as it still might be possible to see roughly when servicing was carried out simply by studying some of the dates, but it's not always easy.

Similarly, if a Pajero has only been in the UK a matter of months, there's no way it can come with any previous MoT certificates to help verify its mileage – so you need to bear this in mind and be extra scrupulous when giving the vehicle the 'once over'.

So, when examining it throughout, not only are you looking for signs of neglect, abuse, accident damage and the like, you're also being vigilant about evidence of non-genuine mileage. If a mileage is indicated at 60,000, for example, you should expect the engine to be reasonably rattle-free (though any old Shogun/Pajero's diesel unit can be clattery when cold, remember), and to emit no excessive smoke when it is revved. The interior should be tidy and not worn, the shock absorbers shouldn't feel too soft or wallowing when cornering, and the bodywork's general condition ought to be in keeping with what might be expected on a vehicle of such mileage. If you have any doubts at all, or the odd alarm bell ringing in your head, it's time to look elsewhere – there's certainly never any shortage of imported Pajeros on sale.

Despite the issue of mileage, most companies specialising in used Pajero imports will be happy to give some kind of a warranty with their vehicles. Depending on the age of the Pajero in question and, of course, what you're paying for it, such warranties can vary from one to three months (or up to six if you're very lucky), and will similarly vary when it comes to their small print and what they may or may not include; you'll need to examine the warranty carefully to satisfy yourself that it's fairly comprehensive. However, at least it should offer some kind of reassurance regarding your chosen Pajero.

In fairness to importers, customers do need to be realistic when discussing the exclusions of any used-car warranty. After all, if you're buying a Series II Pajero

Does the engine in your imported Pajero feel and sound as it should for the mileage? If it seems excessively noisy or is churning out clouds of black smoke, does an indicated mileage of, say, 60,000 seem realistic? Always be on your guard against the many unscrupulous vendors out there. *(Author)*

that's at least a decade old, you can't really expect any warranty that comes with it to be all-encompassing; it will need to take wear and tear into account, and on a 4x4 of such age this is a very wide area for negotiation!

As you've already read in Chapter Five, other issues surrounding imported Pajeros include SVA and ESVA testing, MoT requirements and the like – full details of which can be found in that chapter. However, when looking at any used Pajero for sale, always make sure you check whether it's showing miles or kilometres on its odometer – get this wrong and the impression you've got of the actual mileage could be around 40 per cent out.

Fair wear and tear?

The subject of wear and tear mentioned a couple of paragraphs back doesn't just apply to imported Pajeros, of course; it's just as relevant when it comes to British-

WHAT THE PRESS SAID:
Buying a Series I & II Shogun/Pajero

There are inevitably a few back street car dealers out there who will try to disguise a Pajero's ancestry. If you are in any doubt, there are a handful of obvious giveaways. Mirrors, grilles and door handles are made of 'chrome', and there will be a parking mirror at the end of the nearside front wing. If the original stereo is fitted, the instructions will be in Japanese and will probably make about as much sense as our government's transport policies. Beware!

4x4 Mart, April 2000

Asking an importer or used car dealer to supply a warranty is fine, but be realistic about the small print if the Pajero is 'getting on a bit'. This 1992 Pajero Convertible is hardly likely to come with a cast-iron guarantee. *(Author)*

If you're lucky, the secondhand Shogun/Pajero you're interested in will have enjoyed careful road use only, and not been subjected to the rigours of a farm track every day of its life. More on-road use means less off-road damage. *(Mitsubishi)*

spec Shoguns and, indeed, any other hard-working 4x4. It's perfectly feasible to come across a three-year-old Series III Shogun in immaculate condition that has a low mileage and has never been further off-road than mounting the kerb outside the local delicatessen. Just as with nearly-new Range Rovers, such vehicles are often bought for their head-turning good looks, their status, their street presence and their luxury rather than for any of the off-road or towing benefits they offer.

It's a different story with older Shoguns and Pajeros, most of which will have already gone through several owners during their careers, and most of which will, in some form or another, have worked hard for a living.

Shogun and Pajero usage varies enormously. Yours might be nothing more than a daily user employed for the inevitable school run; on the other hand, it could be a hard-working farmer's tool, a towing vehicle for an extra-large caravan or a holdall for a rural-based builder. Whatever use a vehicle has endured will have had a major effect on its overall condition when you come to view.

Unlike, say, a 20-year-old Suzuki SJ, most Shoguns and Pajeros aren't bought solely as off-road competition or fun machines – which means most haven't had to endure such extreme rough-stuff action. However, a very large proportion of the Shoguns and Pajeros advertised for sale have been used for towing, whether it be a tiny camping trailer or a colossal caravan – and, as with any other vehicle, you need to be aware of the implications of this.

Always try to find out what the vehicle regularly towed, and whether this falls well within its capabilities. If it's an example with manual transmission, does the clutch seem satisfactory? Has the rear suspension been damaged by very heavy towing? Are the rear bumper and the bodywork around the towing bracket in perfect condition, or has the caravan/trailer had a few encounters with these while being hitched to the rear? Use plenty of common sense when viewing such a vehicle, and don't hesitate to say 'No thanks' if you're not happy with the overall condition.

Remember too, that even though most Shoguns and Pajeros aren't bought simply to go mud-plugging, they can still suffer from off-road damage. So, again, carry out all the usual checks that you would with any secondhand 4x4. Is there more mud and debris caked underneath than you'd expected? Are there any signs of dents and damage to the underside of the vehicle? Are the steering, brakes and various suspension components covered in thick mud, suggesting a lack of care? After even the mildest off-roading, any caring owner should thoroughly jet-wash the underside of their 4x4 to prevent any serious build-up of mud. If it looks as though this hasn't taken place, I'd suggest you take a look at another Shogun/Pajero – unless, of course, this example seems spectacularly good value.

As I mentioned earlier, much of this comes down to common sense – and, inevitably, the rules do vary according to the age and price of the vehicle you're interested in purchasing. So if you're spending a modest amount on a Series I Shogun, don't expect pristine bodywork, an immaculate interior and a shiny underside. On the other hand, if you're about to hand over a much more substantial figure for what's described as an excellent Series II, you've every right to expect such niceties. The market always has plentiful supplies of used Shoguns and Pajeros available; it's a case of finding the very best example for your budget.

The good old 2.5-litre turbo-diesel fitted to the Series I
Shogun/Pajero is a phenomenally reliable engine if maintained well
and serviced regularly. Mileages of 200,000-plus aren't uncommon.
(Author)

What goes wrong?

Fortunately, as you'd expect from a product wearing a
Mitsubishi badge, any well maintained Shogun/Pajero
should provide reliable, dependable transport. This is a
major part of the car's appeal, particularly among
buyers who may have been let down by non-Japanese
vehicles over the years. Even so, no 4x4 is truly
invincible – and you need to be prepared before you
jump into Shogun/Pajero ownership for the first time.

Looking specifically at the 1983–91 Series I models
to begin with, the good news is that – despite their age

– they're often still to be found in terrific condition. Any
mechanical woes that may occur will tend to be
connected with ultra-high mileages, so it may be worth
looking around for a lower-mileage example if you've
any doubts. Petrol-engined versions can start to smoke
and have a greater thirst for oil as their miles mount,
although I've heard of several Pajeros over the years
that have successfully completed 200,000-plus miles
each with virtually nothing needed in the way of
major repairs.

The diesel derivatives, despite having the added
complication of a turbocharger, are even more robust,
although it's still worth ensuring the turbo unit itself is
fully functioning before you hand over your cash.
Excessive smoke from a diesel's exhaust can be a sign
of turbo wear – or, if you're lucky, simply a case of worn
injectors. You'll also need to check that, as the revs rise
in each gear, you can feel the turbo spinning into
action; it won't be in the same kind of neck-snapping
way that you'd expect from a turbocharged
performance car, but you should still feel a subtle
increase in acceleration as the turbo starts to do its job.
If you've any doubts, it may be worth getting an
independent inspection carried out before you buy; and
if the vendor claims there's been a new turbo fitted in
the last year or two, insist on seeing a receipt or
guarantee to prove this.

Shogun/Pajero transmissions are generally robust, with synchromesh only starting to fail on mega-mileage examples. Automatic gearboxes can be a little sluggish to change gear when cold, but this isn't necessarily a sign of wear; they're a sturdy and reliable design and will usually outlast the rest of the vehicle.

It's particularly important to thoroughly check the suspension and steering of any Shogun or Pajero you suspect may have been used off-road, as this can obviously accelerate the wear process. If the front ball joints are worn through heavy use or high mileage, these can be expensive to replace; look for signs of uneven tyre wear as an obvious clue. And while we're on the subject of tyres, don't forget to remove the spare wheel cover and check the tread and condition of the spare itself – easily overlooked, even in your determination to be vigilant.

The Mitsubishi's power steering set-up is generally trouble-free, though it's not unusual to see leaks from the power steering box. While you're under there, check for engine and transmission oil leaks, too – not necessarily a major problem depending on your own expectations, but certainly something you should be aware of.

Shogun/Pajero brakes are both straightforward and reliable, though it's not unknown to come across examples with warped front discs. Check this whilst you're taking a look at the whole braking circuit for signs of neglect and wear.

Another major mechanical concern, of course, is the state of the vehicle's dual-range transfer box, so you must ensure it's functioning as it should. Make sure you can select four-wheel drive in both high and low ratios, and then back again to rear-wheel drive without difficulty. Does the relevant '4x4' warning light show up on the dashboard? Do the transfer box changes happen almost instantly, as well as first time every time? You should always try any Shogun/Pajero in all three different drive modes before you agree to buy it, just to ensure it's doing what it was always intended to do. Again, the transfer box itself is a robust, reliable and trustworthy piece of engineering; but years of hard off-road work or a lifetime of regular abuse (perhaps with four-wheel drive being selected at highly inappropriate speeds) can have a long-term negative effect. You can't be too careful.

Body-wise, it's reasonably good news with any Shogun/Pajero – even a very early Series I, as long as it has been well maintained. These vehicles are getting on in years now, so you have to expect signs of old age on

All diesel-engined Shoguns and Pajeros come with the bonus of a turbocharger for extra power, but can you be sure that the turbo is in good working order? If in any doubt, get it checked out before buying the vehicle. *(Author)*

all but the most cosseted examples. However, it's the Pajeros that often show the least signs of age and corrosion, because most have been imported in recent years, which means they haven't had to endure as many British winters and such copious quantities of road salt as a Shogun that has spent all its life in the UK. It's an obvious point, but a relevant one, and during research for this book, I came across far more

Excessive off-road use can play havoc with any 4x4's steering, suspension and braking systems – and the Shogun/Pajero is no exception. Check carefully for obvious signs of abuse or damage. *(Author)*

If a Series I Pajero has only recently been imported into the UK, there's every chance it's in better condition body-wise than a Shogun that has endured a whole life of British winters and road salt. *(Author)*

elderly Shoguns with serious body rot than I did Pajeros suffering from the same disease.

Having said that, I would advise you not to be complacent with any Series I Pajero or Shogun – because any neglected, hard-working 4x4 will eventually

rust. Pay particular attention to the Mitsubishi's front wings (especially just below the indicator unit), rear wheel arches, tailgate, the bottoms of the doors and the sills. And beware of any plastic wheel arch extensions that are fitted, as these can hide serious rust chomping away behind them. Don't assume that a bit of bubbling paintwork is merely that; it's invariably a sign of something far more sinister, and will be the result of rust working its way from the inside outwards.

Above: Other problem areas are the rear corners on each side, just above the bumper wrap-arounds. On this example, the entire lower corner is in the process of completely rotting away. *(Author)*

Right: Front wings are susceptible to rust, particularly around the headlamp area and (as shown here) behind any plastic wheel arch extensions that may be fitted. This Shogun's plastic wheel arch is hiding very severe corrosion. *(Author)*

Right: The bottom of the tailgate is another area to check thoroughly for signs of rust. After a life in the favourable climate of the Canary Islands, this Series I Pajero's is understandably still in superb condition. *(Author)*

Below: Shogun/Pajero sills can get rusty if neglected. This corrosion may look fairly superficial, but a poke with a screwdriver would see a large hole appearing and result in certain MoT failure. *(Author)*

Rust can also break out around the windscreen, a difficult job to have repaired properly; in any case, if a Shogun/Pajero is so rusty round its screen that it needs welding repairs, you have to ask yourself whether the inevitably dubious state of the rest of the vehicle makes the task worthwhile.

It's not unusual to find a rotten floor either, even if the sturdy chassis itself is fairly resilient. It's true that the underside of a Shogun/Pajero is no more rust prone than that of any of its peers, but this can again vary enormously according to the kind of life each vehicle has led. Years of serious off-roading can take their toll if the previous owner hasn't bothered to clean the underside on a regular basis. There are plenty of mud traps under this Mitsubishi to start encouraging the rusting process.

The good news about some of the tatty old Shoguns and Pajeros you may come across is that, despite appearances, they can still be structurally sound. No 4x4 is going to fail its MoT because of surface rust,

paint chips, grazes and scrapes – so if you're not too fussy about cosmetics, you might be able to pick up a bargain. Don't confuse cosmetic tattiness with MoT-failing structural corrosion, though.

The later the better?

When it comes to 1991–2000 Series II Shoguns and Pajeros, the guidelines are not dissimilar to those used for the Series I – but perhaps rather easier to apply. Being later models, these have had less time to deteriorate, corrode or get horrendously abused, which means there are more good examples around.

In fact, there are more examples around of any kind. The Series II Pajero is the model that has flourished most through 'grey' imports over the years, and even now there are plenty still being brought over from Japan. This can be of benefit to you in some ways, because – as mentioned before – the more recently that a secondhand Pajero has been imported, the fewer salt-encrusted British winter roads it has had to endure, and the less chance there's been of serious over-abuse by careless owners. In the main, the Japanese take good care of their cars, and will adhere to service schedules far more rigorously than many Europeans; annual

Series II Shoguns and Pajeros tend to be more resistant to rust than their predecessors. Even so, it pays to carry out the same kinds of checks, as cosmetic and structural corrosion does occur. *(Mitsubishi*

mileages in Japan also tend to be lower than in the UK. It's a major advantage when weighing up the pros and cons of an imported Pajero over a UK-spec Shogun.

Even so, don't be tempted to skimp when it comes to giving any Series II Shogun/Pajero the once-over. In fact, because the basic layout and specification of the Series II are broadly similar in principle to the Series I, it pays to follow the advice I've already given. The good news is that Series II bodywork seems remarkably resilient to rust in all but the most extreme examples (perhaps where a vehicle has previously been accident-damaged and poorly repaired, for example), so you should be pleasantly surprised by what you find, although the previous point about Pajeros being in generally better condition body-wise than Shoguns still applies in many cases.

Don't forget too, that the more recent your Shogun/Pajero is, the more important it will be to focus on its cosmetics, because when the time comes to sell

Rust isn't unheard of with the Series II Pajero; far from it, in fact. The front edge of this badly painted bonnet is showing signs of corrosion, working its way through from the inside. *(Author)*

How important a vehicle's cosmetics are to you will depend on your own priorities and the price you're paying. Use unsightly paintwork like this to bring the price down drastically – if you can live with the looks, of course. *(Author)*

This might look a mess, but a flaking bumper shouldn't cost a fortune to have resprayed – and you could use it to your advantage when haggling to make quite a difference to the price you pay for your Shogun or Pajero. *(Author)*

Battle-scarred or seriously damaged alloys can make any Shogun/Pajero look unsightly. Check closely for early signs of alloy corrosion before you buy. *(Author)*

on the vehicle, it's more likely to be seen by buyers who want a smart-looking example. It's almost to be expected that a 1983 Shogun will be showing a few battle scars by now, so it's less of an issue; but anybody buying a 1993 Series II will expect it to be in far better condition in every sense, not least cosmetically.

Mechanically, despite such changes as increased engine sizes over the years, things are pretty much the same when examining a Series II as when checking a Series I – which means the same levels of reliability in most cases. It's not unusual for early Series II diesels to have injector problems at some stage, which can be pricey to fix; but with the telltale sign being a cloud of thick, black smoke under acceleration, you should spot this when considering such issues as the state of the

WHAT THE PRESS SAID:
Buying a Series II Shogun/Pajero

Residual values are strong because respected 4x4s are always popular, but not all Shoguns make good buys. These cars are often used for towing and off-roading, so careful inspection is recommended before making any purchase. There is also quite a number of grey-import Pajero versions on British roads. While these can provide decent value, they differ from UK spec and aren't worth as much.

Auto Express, September 2002

turbocharger and so on. You also need to inspect the water pump for leaks, as it's not unknown for these to fail prematurely – and that can mean bad news for your engine if its goes unchecked.

So prevalent are imported Series II Pajeros these days, it's more unusual to see a British-spec 1991–2000 Shogun on UK roads than it is to see its Japanese-spec equivalent. This means that if a Series II is your Shogun/Pajero of choice, it's far more likely you'll end up with an import than with an 'official' example – which, cost-wise, isn't a problem. When it comes to spare parts and insurance, for example, things are far easier for owners of imported Pajeros than they were a few years ago – and I'll go into greater detail about this in the next chapter.

Before you buy, do remember to use your common sense when liaising with the vendor. For example, ensure that all duties and VAT were paid when the vehicle was imported, and that you have proof of the Mitsubishi's roadworthiness. This should take the form of an SVA test certificate if one was needed after the Pajero's arrival in the UK (further details of which can be found in Chapter Five), as well as an MoT certificate. You also need to ensure that all the modifications needed to make any Japanese-sourced used car road-legal have been carried out, although these should be covered by a British MoT test – assuming the MoT certificate that comes with the vehicle is genuine, of course.

The vast majority of Pajero importers are good, reputable specialists with an in-depth knowledge of the subject and the expertise to ensure their stock is all road-legal, UK-registered and fully paid for in terms of import duties. If you're unsure for even a second that the person you're thinking of buying a Pajero from can't offer the same kind of reassurance, you know what to do: just walk away.

New generation

By Shogun/Pajero standards, the Series III models of 2000 onwards are relatively new – which means even less to go wrong. And, yes, these later versions have maintained the marque's reputation for world-leading reliability.

Further proof of that came at the end of 2004, when Britain's *Used Car Buyer* magazine voted the Series III Shogun 'Best 4x4' in its annual used car awards. Staff on the magazine were impressed with what they found: 'Despite its bulk and menacing stance, it is easy and pleasant to drive and, with Mitsubishi's impressive

reliability, a three- or four-year-old should feel smooth and tight. The vague steering and bumpy ride of traditional 4x4s are not issues with the current Shogun. The five-speed electronically regulated automatic gearbox is smooth and responsive.'

Indeed, the Series III Shogun's V6 and turbo-diesel engines are, it seems, capable of vast mileages with consummate ease; and the all-new independent suspension all round has also been impressively trouble-free on even the hardest-working examples.

Few Series III Shoguns and Pajeros are bought with hard off-road use in mind, but it pays to carry out the usual checks for tough-terrain damage and excessive wear and tear. Most, though, do end up towing a caravan, boat or horsebox on a regular basis, so you should bear this in mind when examining any used examples.

The Series III Shogun/Pajero has maintained the marque's reputation for reliability, dependability and quality, making any late-model Shogun a tempting buy. *(Mitsubishi)*

Despite its almost unrivalled reputation for durability, the latest-shape Shogun/Pajero hasn't been without its odd difficulty – not least a trio of official recalls to carry out checks and repairs where necessary. These took place in 2001 (affecting 8,800 examples built that year) to replace a faulty brake amplifier; in 2002, following the possibility of a delay problem with the brake servo-assistance; and at the end of 2003, when a problem with the control lever of the cold-start device on certain models resulted in increased engine revs. All of these were dealt with swiftly and effectively, but you need to make sure that any used Series III you're buying has had any required checks and/or

Mitsubishi's latest range of GDI engines is proving a reliable powerplant in high-mileage use. Most British buyers though, opt for the turbo-diesel option – and given the price of fuel in the UK, that's not surprising. *(Author)*

Acres of space and the ultimate in luxury mark out the Series III five-door's interior for particular praise. What a contrast to the more workmanlike interiors of the 1980s... *(Author)*

repair work carried out; it's not impossible for vehicles to slip through the recall net on occasions.

If you're in the market for a late-model used Shogun, you'll be investing a substantially larger sum of money than the buyer of a Series I or Series II example. That means the vehicle you're buying will still be worth a larger proportion of its original list price – which also means it's got further to fall in the future. This might sound obvious (and it is), but depreciation is a far more important factor to bear in mind with a Series III than it is with a Series I or II Shogun/Pajero.

Having said that, this Mitsubishi's overall depreciation levels – and running costs in general – are certainly competitive, as I'll explain in Chapter Eight. Keeping your Shogun/Pajero on the road needn't be a wallet-busting experience.

WHAT THE PRESS SAID:
Buying a Series I & II Shogun/Pajero

There used to be a major shortage of Shoguns on the used market, keeping prices artificially high. With an increase in private imports, supply is no longer such a problem. Prices are slowly falling, and you should be able to shop around for the exact specification you require.

4x4 Mart, April 2000

Running a Shogun or Pajero

Being seen as a premium product has brought Mitsubishi's Shogun and Pajero models mixed blessings, related not only to their running costs but – perhaps more importantly – to the public's perception of running costs. Almost from the start, the Series I Shogun was being described as a cut-price Range Rover; but did this mean that potential owners focused on the 'cut-price' aspect of the description and link it to running costs, or would they have assumed that any Range Rover rival had to cost a fortune to keep on the road?

Reality is often very different from perception, of course, and in this respect, the Shogun/Pajero is no exception. Despite being a premium product that, when new, has often cost more to buy than many of its rivals,

Mitsubishi's most popular 4x4 needn't be prohibitively expensive to keep on (and off) the road these days. As you might expect, much depends on the type and age of Shogun/Pajero you're thinking of buying. So let's start with the most expensive route available to you: buying and running a Series III.

New experiences

As I've explained elsewhere in the book, more recent times have seen latest versions of the Shogun looking

Steady price cuts since the launch of the Series III Shogun have seen the model offering better value than ever in the UK, but if you buy a brand new one, have you considered the cost of depreciation?
(Mitsubishi)

like excellent value for money. Various price cuts throughout the life of the Series III Shogun have brought the model well within reach of large numbers of 4x4 buyers. Happily, this has been achieved without weakening the Shogun's premium image or, indeed, its residuals.

As I mentioned in Chapter Seven, the issue of depreciation is more important to the buyer of a Series III Shogun than to the purchaser of an earlier model, and it's particularly relevant when it comes to buying a brand new one. In fact, is buying new advisable at all, given the weak residuals of so many of today's vehicles?

It depends on your perspective – and the depth of your pockets, of course. For some buyers, nothing but brand new will ever do, so for them the issue of depreciation is an expensive but essential part of their motoring budget. Having said that, I think the situation with the Series III Shogun could be a lot worse. Using figures from 2004, Britain's *Auto Express* magazine gives a good indication of how depreciation eats into a Shogun buyer's budget. Let's take a 3.2-litre Shogun Elegance five-door turbo diesel as an example, a vehicle whose pricing in the UK placed it head-to-head against rivals like the old-style Land Rover Discovery Td5 Landmark, Jeep Grand Cherokee CRD Overland and Volkswagen Touareg TDI Sport. Neither the BMW X5 nor the Mercedes-Benz M-Class were direct competitors, as even their least expensive models cost considerably more than this particular Shogun.

That was quite a tempting choice of upmarket 4x4s, but which one came out on top when it came to obvious running costs. Taking depreciation as the major expense, the Mitsubishi (according to *Auto Express*) would retain an estimated 52 per cent of its list price after three years' ownership. This compared favourably with just 45 per cent residuals for the Land Rover and 43 per cent for the Jeep, but fell behind the Volkswagen at 57 per cent. That was a pretty good showing for the Mitsubishi, and showed that – despite more aggressive pricing as competition increased over the years – the Shogun had maintained its reputation for strong resale values.

Another hefty expense each year with any vehicle in this class can be insurance, and again the results were

Did you know a Shogun 3.2 TD DI-D falls into insurance group 16, compared with group 13 for a 2004-model Land Rover Discovery Td5? Comparing such costs is important before you make a decision as to which vehicle to buy. (Mitsubishi)

a mixed bag when comparing the Shogun with three of its major rivals in 2004. In turbo-diesel long-wheelbase guise, the Mitsubishi carried an insurance rating of Group 16 in the UK, compared with just Group 13 for the Land Rover. The Jeep came in the same grouping as the Shogun, while the VW proved seriously more expensive at Group 19. Whatever your age, occupation or location in the UK, don't underestimate the difference in cost between such diverse insurance groupings – it can add up to quite a chunk of extra expenditure if you don't do your homework in advance.

In every other respect, the Shogun compares favourably with its major rivals, more or less matching them when it comes to the cost of servicing and maintenance. This helps to keep leasing figures for the range very competitive – as do the model's unrivalled reputation for reliability and its impressive lack of warranty claims. Mitsubishi has always provided one of the best new-car warranties on the market, no doubt encouraged by some of the lowest claims in the industry.

Assuming you want a Series III Shogun but you want to reduce the cost of the whole experience, what steps can you take? Most importantly, you can buy used – and this is where some serious savings can come in. Admittedly, the Shogun's residuals are quite impressive by class standards; even so, anybody paying the full new price on such a beast right now can't expect it to be worth much more than half of that in three years' time. The moral of the story? Buy yourself a three-year-old Shogun instead and save yourself a lot of money in the process. Bear in mind, too, that although any secondhand Shogun will continue to fall in value once you've bought it, the most serious depreciation has already taken place during its first three years on the road, which makes the subsequent ownership relatively painless.

Older ... wiser?

By far the most popular Shoguns and Pajeros changing hands on the secondhand scene are from the Series II range of 1991–2000. This is because they're so accessible, both because of the numbers available on the used market and the kind of money they're now fetching.

It's possible nowadays to spend an incredibly small amount of cash buying a used Shogun, especially in the case of a Series I, or an early Series II. Be warned though: at this level, they're not going to be in pristine condition. Far from it, in fact. For a long-wheelbase

You can pick up an elderly Series I Shogun/Pajero quite cheaply these days. But make sure it's structurally sound and always bear in mind how much it may cost to get it through the MoT. Fortunately, this one's a good example. *(Richard Aucock)*

imported Pajero (the most popular variant of the Series II line-up), you'll find yourself paying considerably more, depending on the age, condition and exact specification of the vehicle you're buying. For this though, you can expect a vehicle in extremely good to immaculate condition, well maintained and with a realistically low mileage to its credit.

Pajero values compare favourably with those of major rivals such as the Series I Land Rover Discovery, a 4x4 that is still extremely popular on the used market. With a Pajero, though, you'll find yourself with far more in the way of on-board goodies and standard equipment for your money.

One thing to bear in mind when buying any secondhand Shogun or Pajero is to make sure you're fully aware of its service intervals. These do vary

The cost of buying a Series II varies enormously, a consequence of the model's nine-year production run. Whatever your budget, make sure you buy the very best example you can afford and you shouldn't go far wrong. *(Mitsubishi)*

according to the year of your vehicle and which engine is fitted, so don't be fooled into assuming that any Shogun/Pajero will be fine for another 10,000 miles before it needs a service.

The very earliest Shogun 2.5 TDs had a recommended service interval (or, at the very least, an oil change) of 3000 miles – and, as we'll find out in Chapter Ten, it's very important to adhere to the correct intervals. Of course, you can't guarantee previous owners have been as vigilant, unless you're fortunate enough to have a full service history with your vehicle. But that doesn't mean you can't treat your elderly Shogun/Pajero rather better; a regular oil change makes a significant difference to the condition and long-term reliability of your engine, particularly the diesel units.

Once you've bought your Series I or II Shogun/Pajero though, what about the other expenses: spares, repairs and, particularly when it comes to 'grey' imports, insurance? Again, it's a story with very few nasty surprises.

Spare time

Let's take the issue of parts first – and it's a particularly interesting one. Up until the late 1990s, Mitsubishi's UK importers refused to recognise all the 'unofficial' Pajeros roaming the streets, which meant they wouldn't supply their dealers with any parts specific to the Pajero. This in itself wasn't a massive problem, as so many items were (and still are) interchangeable between Shoguns and Pajeros; but it illustrated the point that if you wanted help or advice from your local Mitsubishi dealer when it came to keeping your Pajero on the road, you were fighting a losing battle.

Mitsubishi then realised it was missing out on a lucrative market and announced it would, after all, be supplying official parts and service items for Japanese-spec Pajeros. Understandably, the company wanted a slice of its own action; it's just a shame it took so long for the decision to be made.

So where does this leave Pajero owners nowadays? With rather more choice, is the obvious answer. In theory, you can go along to any Mitsubishi dealer and order any parts still available for your particular Japanese-spec Pajero. And, generally, the prices are competitive. The myth that every part for every Japanese vehicle is prohibitively expensive is finally starting to be recognised as nonsense.

If you don't want to deal with official franchised dealers, don't worry. There are large numbers of Japanese 4x4 specialists in the UK (and, indeed,

A diesel-engined Shogun or Pajero requires more regular servicing than a petrol-powered example. On the other hand, the difference in fuel consumption usually more than makes up for this... *(Author)*

throughout Europe) keen to help you in your search for parts and accessories for all Shoguns and Pajeros – whatever their age, spec or exact model. In the main, such companies offer an excellent service and keen prices.

Whether you're in the market for spares right now or you're simply interested in finding out more about prices at this stage, I'd recommend you take a look at the websites offered by some of these specialists – a comprehensive list of which appears in Appendix A. It can make fascinating reading, and it certainly proves the point that running a Pajero needn't be any more expensive than owning a Shogun.

Nowadays there's a wide choice of outlets selling spares and accessories for all Shoguns and Pajeros. The best of these specialists offer a superb service and extremely competitive prices. *(Author)*

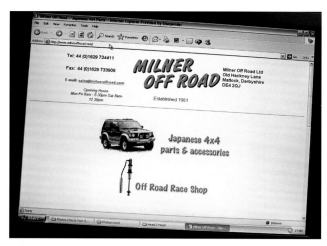

Independent specialists in spares and accessories for 4x4s can easily be found throughout the UK. Check out some of the websites listed in Appendix A and start comparing prices. You might just be pleasantly surprised. *(Author)*

You will find on these websites all the parts and accessories you're likely to need and they are often competitively priced. Parts common to both Shoguns and Pajeros are easily identified, and items such as oil filters, radiator top hoses or cam belts can be found at very reasonable prices, if you shop around.

Even the larger parts, such as heavy-duty rear shock absorbers, rear leaf springs or water pumps may not break the bank, if you do a bit of research on the web before you buy. I'd go as far as to say that maintaining or repairing a Shogun or Pajero of 1983–2000 vintage needn't be any more expensive than doing the same with an early Land Rover Discovery. When you think how many Land Rover specialists there are in the UK, which means intense competition between them all, that's quite an achievement. Don't be misled into assuming that a large, Japanese-built 4x4 is going to bankrupt you every time it needs a service or some kind of repair work; it simply isn't the case.

Don't forget that whenever you're ordering parts or accessories, it's important you stress whether your particular vehicle is a Shogun or a Pajero. Although huge numbers of parts are interchangeable, minor differences in specification mean you can't always assume this is the case. Talk to your parts supplier; explain the exact model, engine and specification level, and you should have no difficulties.

Insurance issues

Insurance can be another matter, although the situation has improved significantly over the years. It's not very long ago that most mainstream insurers wouldn't consider offering cover on a Pajero 'grey' import. Happily, they have been forced to adapt to market changes and, anxious not to lose any business, most will now insure just about any Pajero.

No longer are you forced, it seems, to seek help from a specialist broker when insuring a Pajero – but we wanted to put this to the test. We therefore contacted six mainstream car insurance companies (including the UK market leader Direct Line) and asked about insurance in relation to both Shoguns and Pajeros; and the results were very interesting.

Every mainstream company we spoke to would indeed insure the 1994 Pajero 2.8 TD we explained we were interested in. However, most also insisted it had to be fitted with a Thatcham-approved immobiliser (and they would need proof of this via a fitter's certificate), a requirement that wasn't insisted on if we were insuring a Shogun of similar specification.

As for the actual premiums, the exercise proved that although insuring a Pajero isn't difficult, it can be expensive depending on your personal circumstances. From our half-dozen mainstream companies, all of them quoted a higher premium for a 1994 Pajero than for a Shogun of the same age and similar spec – with the smallest gap coming in at a 25 per cent difference. In one instance, the Pajero was 60 per cent dearer to insure than the 'official' Shogun.

In every case too, the insurers insisted on a higher excess (the first part of any claim that you pay for yourself) with a Pajero than with a Shogun. Admittedly, the difference isn't huge, but it's something to bear in mind when shopping around for insurance.

Keen to find out whether such extra expenses were merely a feature of the larger insurance companies, we then spoke to specialist brokers Adrian Flux, a very successful organisation offering cover for all sorts of specific market sectors – including classic cars, 4x4s, custom cars and many others. The result? Yes, in most circumstances, a Pajero will be between 30 and 50 per cent more expensive to insure than a Shogun, although the process of actually gaining insurance cover isn't difficult.

So why does this extra expense exist? For a variety of reasons. Pajeros, it seems, are statistically more likely to be stolen or involved in accidents than Shoguns. (There's no obvious, logical reason for this – but since when did statistics take logic into account?) Pajeros also tend to be better equipped and cosmetically more complicated, which means even a minor shunt can

involve the replacement of more trim, trickier paint schemes and the like. Whatever the reasons for the difference, there's very little you can do about it.

Except, that is, for the ridiculous course of action that some owners of 'grey' imports have tried over the years. They have assumed that by swapping their Pajero's badges for a Shogun's they could insure their vehicle as the latter rather than the former. This is foolish, so don't ever be tempted to follow suit! The registration document still says Pajero, the specification is still very much Pajero – and if ever you were obliged to make a claim, your insurance company's assessors are sufficiently well trained to spot a Pajero over a Shogun from twenty paces. If it's a Pajero you're driving, make sure it's a Pajero you're insuring.

In any case, it's important to keep this whole issue of insurance in perspective. Unless you're an 18 year old, have a string of motoring convictions, live in an inner city and your vehicle is left in the street all night, your insurance premium is still likely to be affordable. I'd just recommend that you do a little research and get a few quotes before you take the plunge into Shogun/Pajero ownership. It makes sense, doesn't it?

You might think a Series II Pajero is almost identical to a Series II Shogun. Even so, the former will cost up to 50 per cent more to insure than the latter. As ever, it pays to shop around. *(Author)*

You can probably afford to buy the Shogun/Pajero of your dreams – but can you afford to insure it? Do your homework and get a few specific quotes before you agree to any purchase. *(Author)*

Chapter Nine

Mods and upgrades

There's no doubt that the Mitsubishi Shogun/Pajero appeals to a different kind of enthusiast from those of the old Land Rovers and Suzuki SJs of this world. Each

So this might be a bit over the top for pottering to the shops – even in downtown Dakar. But if you want to make your Shogun/Pajero a tad better off-road, there's plenty that can be done without spending a fortune. *(Mitsubishi)*

of the latter is usually bought by off-road fanatics keen to spend extra money on modifications that will make these machines even more formidable in off-road use. But the Shogun/Pajero is rarely bought purely as an off-road fun machine.

It's not that the Shogun/Pajero isn't an off-roader, of course; it's simply that reliable everyday on-road usage is also usually part of an owner's requirements. Let's

face it, Suzuki SJs are usually owned purely for off-road fun nowadays; such activity is rarely the sole reason for owning a Shogun or Pajero.

Heading off-road

Assuming that you'd like your Mitsubishi to be able to cope with the rough stuff when the need arises, how much work do you need to carry out in the way of modifications? Well, how far you go with any mods depends on how much time and money you want to invest in the project, as well as how seriously you're likely to take your off-roading.

Rest assured that even a basic Shogun or Pajero is capable of getting you through some reasonably tough terrain. In fact, there's absolutely no reason why you shouldn't take any (preferably short-wheelbase) Shogun or Pajero off-road and have a lot of fun in it, without carrying out any modifications whatsoever. But if you're likely to be off-roading on a regular basis, some basic changes are certainly advisable.

For a start, have a look at the tyres on your Mitsubishi. Are they the standard road tyres you'll find on most Shoguns and Pajeros? If so, they're likely to prove less than perfect in off-road conditions. You need maximum grip, and a standard set of rubber just isn't up to the job. Talk to some of the 4x4 specialist companies we've listed in Appendix A and ask them what the optimum choice of tyre is for your model. Tell them how much of your driving is likely to be off-road; how important (or not) on-road comfort is to you; and also what kind of a budget you have to play with. They'll then be able to come up with the ideal compromise for your particular needs. It's not rocket science, but the perfect choice of tyre will vary between different series of Shoguns/Pajeros and different owners. Get the right set of rubber on your Mitsubishi and, we promise you, you'll be amazed at the difference in grip and go-anywhere capabilities.

Off-road tyres will certainly get you places you

You can take any Shogun/Pajero off-road in completely standard form, and will probably find it more than adequate for your needs. But even the most basic modifications can make quite a difference.
(Richard Aucock)

Changing the tyres on your Mitsubishi can make a massive difference to its off-road prowess. But you need to get the compromise right, depending on whether you'll be off-roading regularly or only occasionally. Do you really have to fit 'all-terrain' tyres for your particular needs? *(Author)*

couldn't have reached beforehand, but you don't want to ruin your engine getting there, so an engine snorkel of some description is advisable for serious off-roading. This ensures the air intake for your vehicle is higher than any water you're likely to be wading through, which is handy when it comes to preventing your engine from seizing up! That's why you see lots of off-roaders around with snorkels running up the side of their windscreens, although whether you'll be happy cutting a hole in one of your front wings for the snorkel to exit through is another matter.

While you're at it, sealing your electrical system is also advisable, with a waterproof distributor cap and plug leads being particularly useful in very tough conditions. For most owners, it's not that important; but for the avid off-roader, it's worth considering.

If all this sounds rather 'over the top', it's probably because you're not the kind of owner who will be off-roading in any serious way on a regular basis. On the other hand, why not make the most of the capabilities your vehicle already has, and improve them just a little? You might then find you're tempted to go off-road in a way that had never occurred to you before.

You may even want to start thinking along the lines of modified suspension. This involves more expenditure than a set of off-road tyres; but with the benefits to be gained, it can be worthwhile, and not just when off-roading. Invest in a set of uprated leaf springs, for example, and you'll have a more robust off-roader on your hands, as well as a vehicle even more capable when towing a heavy trailer, caravan or horsebox.

Various specialists are able to supply uprated shock absorbers, which can again improve the off-road experience – even if there is a risk of a harsher on-road ride. Some companies will even supply suspension lift kits for certain models of Shoguns/Pajeros. If that sounds as though it might be a hefty investment, it could be money well spent when you consider that you will gain an extra 40mm or so of ground clearance

An on-road tyre like this will be pretty useless in the rough, particularly once the tread has filled with mud. Also, check out that seriously uneven tyre wear – probably the result of the steering being knocked out of line whilst off-roading in the past. *(Author)*

(quite important for the serious off-roaders). Do remember, though, that a suspension lift kit fitted to any 4x4 will affect the on-road driving characteristics, so you need to decide what's more relevant to your needs: extra clearance for tough-terrain challenges or a first class on-road drive?

Whatever your off-road requirements, take a look at some of the websites featured in Appendix A and see what's on offer from the many 4x4 specialists we've listed. Always think of your own particular needs and expectations, and don't hesitate to ask specialists for advice; they're there to help, and most of them are only too willing to pass on their expertise to a potential customer. Remember that it's your money you're spending, and whatever amount you set aside for off-road modifications won't all be recouped when you come to sell your vehicle. If you're only a very occasional off-roader, is it really worth spending so much to transform your Shogun/Pajero into a jungle warrior? It's your call.

Before heading off-road in your Mitsubishi, don't forget to stock up on essentials to get yourself away from trouble when you're out 'in the rough'. At the very least, you'll need some decent boots, a pair of gloves, wheel-changing equipment, a good quality tow rope, some spare petrol, a full water container and a basic

Want to go further? Looking to upgrade your suspension, perhaps? Perusing the specialists' websites will give you a clear idea of exactly what's available for your model. *(Author)*

If you're about to embark on a spot of off-roading, make sure your Shogun/Pajero is complete with some essential pieces of kit. Pack a tow rope, spare water, a basic tool kit and so on – you never know when you'll need them. *(Richard Aucock)*

tool kit that includes spare fuses, wire, bulbs, a can of WD40 and so on. Failing to prepare yourself in such a way is foolhardy, to say the least. When off-roading in a group or taking part in a 4x4 fun day, there's usually plenty of help around from other willing volunteers; but don't assume there'll always be someone else with a tow rope or a tool kit you can use.

One final point about equipment: many off-road enthusiasts are now fitting electric front winches to their vehicles, an excellent idea if you're going to be off-roading most weekends and likely to be pushing your Shogun or Pajero to the limit. Being able to winch yourself up a crazily steep incline or out of a mud bath that proved more than a match for your Mitsubishi can be both useful and pretty good fun. It makes you more

Taking part in 4x4 fun days can be a great way of getting to know your vehicle's and your own capabilities. If you simply want to enjoy the gentlest parts of the course like this, it's no problem. You're there to have fun, not to compete. *(Richard Aucock)*

self-sufficient too, should there be a lack of help about. But do shop around and talk to 4x4 specialists about the ideal winch for your particular needs; prices and specifications vary greatly, but there is a wide range of winches available to suit most pockets. Do your homework thoroughly; you might just avoid spending more money than you need to.

Out in the rough

I won't bother going into intricate detail here about the various different types of off-road competitions that exist for those already heavily involved in the sport. Whether you're into trialling or comp safari events, you'll already have spent a serious amount of money preparing your vehicle, you'll be a member of the various clubs and organisations that organise the sports, and you'll have gone much further in the preparation of your 4x4 than most readers of this book.

For the rest of us, who tend to look upon off-roading as a non-competitive fun activity for the weekend, there

What do you want to achieve with your add-ons and accessories? It's relatively easy to make any Shogun/Pajero – or, in this instance, L200 – look cool on the street with lots of chrome and some smart alloys and tyres. How far do you go? Much depends on your budget.
(Mitsubishi)

are now lots of new opportunities to get our Shoguns and Pajeros dirty. More off-road driving schools than ever before are now established throughout the UK, and 4x4 fun days are becoming increasingly popular, too.

How the latter work is very simple. You turn up on the day at a specially designated site (often an old quarry), you pay your fee (usually between £30 and £45), you sign a disclaimer (acknowledging that you and you alone are responsible for your vehicle and your personal safety) … and then you spend the next few hours having fun.

First-timers at most 4x4 fun days will find help and advice available to them if they so wish. An expert will usually be on hand to give you basic instruction on off-roading, and they will often accompany you on a trip round the course if you ask them to, so you can get acquainted with the layout and what's on offer.

The whole point about off-road fun days is that there's no competition involved. The only person you're up against (in terms of how hard you push your vehicle) is yourself. Whether you're the kind of owner who wants to potter round the perimeter of the site and practice on the easy sections, or you're the more adventurous fanatic who likes nothing more than powering your modified Mitsubishi through a lake just for the sheer hell of it, you'll be made equally welcome at any fun day.

There are no competitions, prizes or winners; you're there just to have fun. And if that's what you're into, do

make sure that it's either as part of a properly organised fun day or, if you're 'going your own way', you have the land owner's full permission. There's a lot of controversy at the time of writing about off-roaders using 'green lanes' and other public spaces to put their vehicles through their paces, much to the annoyance of ramblers, cyclists, horse riders and the like. Whatever we, individually, may think about such opinions, we need to be aware of other land users. In recent years, less responsible 4x4 owners have helped to spoil the reputation of off-roaders amongst the public at large.

That's why I recommend 4x4 fun days as the ideal compromise. By talking to some of the off-road organisers listed in Appendix A, you'll be able to find out what's coming up in your area over the next few months. Go on, have fun!

Back on dry land

If the first part of this chapter doesn't seem to apply particularly to you, that's because you're not an off-road addict. Which is absolutely fine. Just because you own a 4x4 – even one of the best, like the Shogun/Pajero – doesn't mean you have to head for the

Specialist 4x4 breakers' yards can be a great source of parts and accessories at reasonable prices. A secondhand bull bar would cost far less than a new one, but may need repainting to make perfect; worth the effort, surely? *(Author)*

hills or find yourself wading through mud at the first opportunity. Keeping a 4x4 primarily for on-road use, though, doesn't mean your vehicle won't benefit from some modifications. And it all starts with aesthetics.

Whichever series of Shogun/Pajero (or Pinin, Challenger or L200) you own, there's no shortage of

A 'proper' Pajero fog lamp adorns the front end of a write-off in a breaker's yard. It's not in perfect condition, but it was going cheap. *(Author)*

extras and accessories on the market to make it look a whole lot better. But before you start reaching for your credit card, have a serious think about what you're trying to achieve. Are you after a smarter on-road look? Do you want to make your Shogun/Pajero look a tad more rugged? Or perhaps you're simply after some extra luxury and a more upmarket feel? Think which of these applies to you, because what you spend your hard-earned cash on will vary depending on your answer.

Bargain breakers

Before we talk more specifically about what's available, do bear in mind there's an increasing number of specialist breakers in the UK these days, offering good quality used parts for Japanese vehicles. Again, take a look at Appendix A for details of some of the best-known Japanese vehicle dismantlers. These are the companies that buy accident-damaged cars, trucks and 4x4s, strip them for spares and then sell off whatever is of value, and they can be a great source of accessories and upgrades.

One word of warning (which should be common sense but I'll mention it anyway) concerns safety. Under no circumstances should you ever consider buying any used items that are critical to the safety of your Shogun/Pajero when the donor vehicle has been involved in an accident. Don't be tempted to cut corners and fit a set of secondhand shock absorbers, tyres or steering components (just three of the most obvious examples) from a write-off when the future performance of such items may well have been compromised by the impact.

Where breakers can be extremely useful though, is when it comes to upgrades and accessories. You fancy a front bull bar for your Pajero? It will be cheaper to buy a used example from a breaker; it might need repainting if it's been around for a few years, but the money you save should make that worthwhile. You want to upgrade your British-spec Series I Shogun's interior to an all-leather Japanese-spec Pajero's? Again, get in touch with one of the specialist breakers and you might be surprised at just what's available.

Base-model Shoguns and Pajeros can certainly benefit from interior and exterior upgrades, and the secondhand option is often the way to go. Your particular early Shogun might not have 'chrome' door mirrors, for example, but a Pajero in a breaker's yard almost certainly will. And it's the same with so many items of trim and various accessories, both internal and external. Check out what's around and keep an eye on the specialists' websites; there are some bargains to be had.

Cool new look

Enhancing the appearance and styling of your Shogun/Pajero purely for road use isn't especially difficult – and it can be great fun. Again, refer to Appendix A for full contact details of some of the most successful Shogun/Pajero and general 4x4 specialists around. If you're anything like me, you'll be happy spending the odd hour or two perusing their websites to see just what's available for your model. Often among the most popular choices of upgrade is a replacement set of alloy wheels, with a bewildering array of different styles on the market. Your final choice will invariably be decided by a combination of aesthetic preference and what you're willing to spend. Always remember, though, that alloys require more maintenance than standard steel wheels, and are also more susceptible to damage; so if you regularly go off-road or your Shogun/Pajero is often used for towing a horsebox through seriously muddy fields, is a shiny new set of alloys likely to be the wisest of investments?

An attractive set of alloys like this... *(Richard Aucock)*

...can transform the look of any Shogun/Pajero. If you're a regular off-roader though, is it a wise decision? Alloy wheels need more maintenance and are less robust than plain steel ones.

(Richard Aucock)

A strong and robust bull bar – like this Series I item – is still a popular choice for many Shogun/Pajero owners. *(Japanese 4x4 Spares)*

For 'street' use, other popular upgrades include alloy side steps (often fitted as standard on Japanese-spec Pajeros), chrome-effect spare wheel covers and, of course, front bull bars or A-bars.

The more subtle approach of an A-bar is fast catching on with many enthusiasts. A wide range of style and materials is on offer from some of the specialists listed in this book. *(Richard Aucock)*

The whole subject of bull bars has caused controversy since the mid-1990s, when the issue of pedestrian safety really started to emerge. Claims were made in the press that any pedestrian struck by a large 4x4 with a bull bar fitted was likely to suffer far greater injuries and had a higher chance of being killed than somebody hit by a 'normal' car. These claims are still made today.

Whatever the facts in this matter, bull bars are still legal in the UK and are a popular 4x4 fashion accessory. Many owners cite their sheer usefulness as a reason for fitting them, too: the car park knocks that seem to be a part of modern-day driving are, they argue, less likely to occur when your 4x4 has an enormous bull bar adorning its front end. And that certainly makes some sense.

How's this for one-upmanship? A chrome ladder for climbing up onto your Shogun/Pajero's roof rack might seem a bit over the top (excuse the pun) … but it's actually very practical. *(Richard Aucock)*

So … will you be fitting bull bars to your Shogun/Pajero? It's your decision, and I'm not here to influence you either way. If pedestrian safety is of major concern to you, it's worth looking into the availability of some of the more pedestrian-friendly A-bars that are now available through specialists. But if a bull bar is top of your list of requirements … well, there's no denying that they do look good. They give any Shogun/Pajero a certain 'attitude', particularly with a chrome finish. Decisions, decisions…

The official route

When deciding on styling upgrades and enhancements for your Shogun or Pajero, don't forget the official lines of accessories available via Mitsubishi themselves. Any Mitsubishi dealer will be able to supply you with an accessories catalogue for the 2000-onwards Shogun range, as well as for the Pinin, Shogun Sport and L200; but even if you own an older Shogun/Pajero, you can still go the 'official' route if you want to.

Getting hold of an old accessories catalogue for the Series I and II Shoguns/Pajeros can be good fun; you still see them for sale (often at bargain prices) at autojumbles and the like. That way, you can research what was available for your model when it was brand new, and then embark upon trying to find as many new-old-stock or secondhand items as you can.

My own early accessories catalogues for the Shogun feature such tempting goodies as a wheel arch and body moulding kit, front and rear lamp protectors, an off-road lamp bar, an interior wood-veneer trim kit and lots more. Some of these items may well be fitted to Shoguns/Pajeros that can now be found in breakers' yards. Alternatively, 4x4 magazines and even the eBay auction website can be good sources of privately advertised items that people no longer want.

Extra power

Seriously boosting the power of your Shogun/Pajero is an interesting subject area, albeit one that should be approached with caution. Previous chapters have pointed out that the earliest turbo-diesel Shoguns were almost sloth-like in their performance compared with later models; so if power and acceleration are of paramount importance to you, we can only assume you won't be buying a diesel-engined Series I in the first place.

Shogun and Pajero owners aren't renowned for having tarmac-burning performance at the top of their list of requirements. If, however, you have a greater

Collecting old brochures and accessories catalogues for early models can be good fun − as can collecting some of the period accessories within them! Not sure about the sleeveless Shogun jacket, though…
(Mitsubishi)

need for speed than most owners, a petrol-engined Shogun/Pajero would seem to be the way to go. In both Series I and II guises, the V6 models offer impressive on-road performance and a healthy turn of speed – all at the expense of fuel economy, of course. On the other hand, you might be lucky enough to find a Shogun/Pajero V6 advertised that has already had an LPG conversion carried out, effectively reducing your fuel bill by as much as half without drastically affecting the performance. You can have just about any petrol-powered Shogun/Pajero converted to LPG, but it won't be cheap if you have a professional job done; and unless you're intent on keeping your vehicle indefinitely or you cover a huge annual mileage, you need to ask yourself whether such an investment is actually worthwhile.

Turbo-diesel 4x4s of just about any description can be improved upon, of course – but much depends on your priorities. For the biggest boost in performance without sacrificing the long-term reliability of your

Fancy a boost to your Shogun/Pajero turbo diesel's power and performance? British company Bromleys offer a Tunit device claimed to increase brake-horsepower by as much as 30 per cent. *(Bromleys)*

Shogun/Pajero, it might be worth investing in something like a Tunit – a relatively simple device that boosts the power of a diesel engine by up to 30 per cent. Produced and sold direct by UK-based Bromleys, Tunits are available for 2.5- and 3.2-litre direct-injection diesel-engined Shoguns and Pajeros, as well as 2.5-litre L200s. More applications are continually being added to the range, so contact Bromleys direct to find out the latest information.

The claims made for Mitsubishis fitted with Tunits are impressive. A 3.2-litre Shogun DI-D, for example, is said to have its power boosted from 160 to 180bhp, while torque is increased from 276 to a massive 307lb ft. Similarly, a 2001-model L200 2.5 TD is said to see power increased to 120bhp (from just 100bhp), with torque boosted significantly from 178 to 207lb ft. Not only does the extra power prove useful out on the

street, but such a noticeable gain in torque also comes into its own when off-roading. The cost of a Tunit varies from model to model, so you will need to talk to the manufacturer about your requirements, but it is unlikely to be an excessive amount for so useful a boost in performance.

It's also worth speaking with Van Aaken. They manufacture and market the Van Aaken SmartBox, a programmable digital device that claims to accurately alter fuelling and injection timing to give substantial gains in both power and torque. These changes are fully mapped across the load and RPM range to give what Van Aaken describes as '…excellent driveability and control while providing maximum power with minimal smoke'.

With a range of SmartBox (for electronic turbo-diesels) and SmartPower (for mechanical turbo-diesels) add-ons now available, Van Aaken can take just about any diesel-powered Shogun, Pajero, Challenger or L200 and give it some vital extra 'oomph' – in both bhp and torque. This results in diesel-powered machines with more 'driveability' – more power, more torque, fewer gear changes and a generally superior driving experience.

If you don't want to go that far but you do want to make the most of what your Mitsubishi already has, there are some simpler options available to you. For example, talk to any 4x4 specialist about the availability of special air filters for your vehicle that will offer a more effective filtration than a standard filter, but,

Right: Depending on the age and model of Shogun/Pajero you own, a Van Aaken SmartBox or SmartPower device should give a major boost to your vehicle's power output, outright performance and torque levels. All very useful stuff, both on- and off-road. *(Van Aaken)*

Below: Several companies claim to be experts at boosting diesel performance. Berkshire-based Van Aaken Developments is one of the most respected in its field. *(Author)*

thanks to their enhanced airflow, will also provide a useful (albeit slight) increase in power output, as well as improved fuel consumption.

Whatever you do to your Shogun/Pajero to improve its performance, the vehicle will only ever be as good as the sum of its parts – which means there's little point spending hundreds of pounds on power upgrades if the engine has already covered a quarter of a million miles and the turbocharger is showing serious signs of old age. Be sensible in your expectations, and seek an effective improvement to any aspect of your Mitsubishi's performance only if it's already a healthy and well-maintained example.

How far do you go?

Whatever the reason for modifying your Shogun or Pajero, and no matter what you're trying to achieve at the end of it all, the best advice is to keep a firm grasp on reality at all times. With a credit card in your hand and an accessories catalogue or website right in front of you, it's very easy to get carried away and spend a not-so-small fortune on add-ons and improvements for your Shogun or Pajero.

So how much of all this do you actually need? And, if you're about to spend a sizeable sum on improving the performance and handling of an old Series I, wouldn't you be better off – and have an easier life – if you simply bought a more powerful Series II instead?

These are all personal decisions, and just how far you go with modifying your Shogun/Pajero is down to you. Just remember that whatever you spend on improvements won't add anywhere near the same amount to the value of your vehicle. Invest only in upgrades that are going to be genuinely useful to you, and you won't go far wrong.

Bear in mind how much you're spending when you embark on modifications to your Shogun/Pajero (or Shogun Pinin, as shown here), and always bear in mind your vehicle's resale value. The best advice? Go and have fun! *(Safety Devices)*

Chapter Ten

Looking after your Mitsubishi

Whether you choose a Series I, II or III Shogun/Pajero, how you maintain it and look after it will have a crucial influence on its overall condition when you eventually come to sell it. However, because of the wide variety of different specifications, powerplants and derivatives available over the years, it would be impossible to go

If you own a Series I or II Shogun/Pajero, getting hold of a Haynes Workshop Manual for your vehicle is essential. It's packed full of invaluable advice and step-by-step procedures for maintaining and repairing your Mitsubishi. *(Author)*

into great detail here about every aspect of maintenance for every version produced.

For owners of earlier Shoguns and Pajeros, Haynes does produce a specific workshop manual. Originally published in 1994, it covers Series I and II Shoguns, as well as the earlier L200 pick-ups. Although of American origin, which means lots of references to the model are in the name of Montero rather than Shogun or Pajero, it is still extremely useful to owners in the UK and throughout Europe.

This manual can be ordered from any retail book outlet (by quoting ISBN number 1 85010 944 3) or direct from Haynes. For telephone orders, call 01963 442030; or check out the company's website at www.haynes.co.uk for details of online ordering.

Happily, given the fairly straightforward technical specifications of most members of the Shogun/Pajero family, much of the basic maintenance of these all-wheel-drive Mitsubishis applies equally to other 4x4s – so I'll attempt to deal with as much of this as possible.

Routine maintenance

The most obvious advice when talking about basic maintenance is: do make sure you adhere to the manufacturer's recommended service intervals. This applies as much to a well-worn Series I Pajero as it does to a nearly new Shogun Warrior; whatever the age or spec of your Mitsubishi, regular servicing is an absolute must, particularly if you're a keen off-roader.

Fail to change the oil in your engine when you should, for example, and over time you'll find yourself up against premature engine wear and extra long-term expense. Furthermore, if you're an avid off-road fan and like nothing more than pushing your Shogun/Pajero to the limit in the rough, you'll find yourself going through sets of brake pads, alternators, batteries and the like far more frequently than the average tarmac-only motorist. Although Mitsubishis tend to be inherently reliable, any kind of hard off-road work puts extra pressure on key components, which means more regular checks and maintenance should soon become second nature to you.

Much of the very basic maintenance that goes with regular off-roading boils down to common sense. In extreme off-road conditions, for example, it's not unusual for radiators to get caked in mud which, once dried, hugely restricts airflow and can cause overheating, which in turn can cause major engine damage if left unchecked. The simple answer is to keep your radiator as clean as possible with regular jet-washing, which will help prolong the life of both the radiator and everything else affected by the cooling system. In fact, keeping the whole of your under-bonnet area clean and free from any serious build-up of mud will be beneficial in the long run.

A good hosing down of your brakes is important after off-roading, too. A build-up of sand or mud will not only make your brakes less effective and potentially dangerous on the road, but can also deeply score your brake discs. Go off-roading in an old quarry, for example, and you may find the sand there is very abrasive and damaging. The sooner you can remove all traces of it afterwards, the more your Mitsubishi will benefit.

While you're out with your jet wash, don't forget to make full use of it underneath your Shogun/Pajero, too. A regular build-up of mud will often cause bodywork problems later on; most 4x4s have a whole host of mud

Keeping your engine this clean isn't always easy, but after serious off-roading, it's essential you wash any caked-on mud away from your radiator and other ancillaries; it will increase the longevity of many key components along the way. *(Author)*

Jet-washing the underside of your Mitsubishi on a regular basis is good advice, especially if you tend to go 'mud plugging' every so often. It will help prevent corrosion underneath, as well as keeping suspension, steering and brakes free of mud, silt and general off-road crud. *(Author)*

traps and nooks and crannies just waiting to catch debris, moisture and whatever else off-roading throws at them. Neglect the underside and, eventually, you'll find rust setting in – a subject I'll come to a little further on in this chapter.

Whether or not you go off-roading in your Mitsubishi, it's vital that you carry out regular checks of the under-bonnet essentials. These obviously include the engine oil and coolant levels on a weekly basis. However, don't neglect your brake fluid level – particularly vital if you've been over rough terrain, as it's easy to damage a brake hydraulic line and not realise it until you encounter an on-road emergency. If you suspect you have a brake fluid leak, don't drive the vehicle; have it checked out immediately, for obvious reasons. As part of your maintenance regime, don't forget such areas as the transmission fluid and power steering fluid levels; they're both generally reliable and need little attention, but leaks are not unknown.

When checking out any Shogun/Pajero that's for sale, you should ensure that all its electrical and electronic items are working as they should. But what happens if electrical woes occur after you've bought the vehicle?

Despite a proliferation of electrical gadgets on Pajero Exceeds in particular, any Shogun/Pajero's electrics are generally very reliable. Electric windows and electrically adjustable door mirrors are rarely non-functioning, although if they are, repairs are usually straightforward. *(Author)*

The best advice is not to panic. Mitsubishi's electrical systems are generally very reliable and long lasting, which will no doubt come as a relief to anybody caught out by the electrical problems experienced by many of the earliest Land Rover Discoverys, for example. Even better news is that electrical problems are often less complicated and less expensive than you might assume; so make sure you check for a blown fuse, a wire that's come adrift or a faulty earth connection before assuming that a whole electric window mechanism (or whatever) needs replacing.

We've previously talked about the importance of buying a Shogun/Pajero with a full service history where feasible; well, the continuation of this history is equally vital once you've bought your vehicle. Even if you choose to use a small independent garage rather than a Mitsubishi-franchised dealer for your maintenance and servicing, there's no reason why they can't keep your service book up to date and stamped. When you come to sell your Shogun/Pajero, it will be well worthwhile; buyers are always impressed by evidence of regular servicing and a high standard of maintenance.

Even if you've bought a recently imported Pajero with no service history (or, at best, one written in Japanese), don't think you're wasting your time by starting to build a 'new' service history from scratch. If you keep your Mitsubishi two or three years and subsequent potential owners can see you've had it serviced as and when it should have been, you're far more likely to get the price you're hoping for. Even a vehicle as renowned for reliability as a Mitsubishi Pajero will benefit from having even just a partial service history, and subsequent buyers will be more impressed than ever if you've kept receipts for work carried out, repairs commissioned or even just parts bought during your period of ownership. It all helps to build the impression that you genuinely look after your vehicle – which, of course, you do.

When going through any vehicle's history, don't forget to check when (or indeed, if) it last had its cam belt changed. If you've already acquired the vehicle and you can find no record of a new cam belt, don't delay: get your vehicle booked in for the job as soon as possible. If the worst happens and your cam belt snaps, you'll be very lucky to escape with anything less than a full engine rebuild or even a replacement. If you're thinking of buying a Shogun/Pajero that hasn't yet had its cam belt changed, make sure you budget this into the price when negotiating with the vendor.

Bodywork care

Previous chapters have already dealt with the fact that, despite being well built and robust, any old Shogun or Pajero that isn't exactly cherished can eventually start to show signs of rust. They're made from steel, after all, and they're not going to last forever. There is much that you, as an owner, can do to at least slow down the corrosion process, though.

For a start, think about investing in a DIY pressure washer if you haven't already got one. These needn't be expensive, yet they're hugely useful to anybody who owns a 4x4 that leads an active life.

Whenever you head off-road and encounter the usual combination of mud, water, slurry, sand and the like, use your pressure washer when you get home to remove as much of this as you can before it dries hard. You only need to glance underneath your Mitsubishi to realise there's no shortage of areas where such debris can get trapped: all around the chassis members; up inside the wheel arches; behind light units; around box sections ... and a whole lot more.

Combine this with the corrosive road salt that local councils drop on the streets every winter and you've got an undesirable cocktail of rust-inducing 'rubbish' accumulated under your vehicle.

If you're very keen, you might even want to think about investing in some kind of rust-prevention treatment. Products such as Waxoyl can be applied either by brush or sprayed into hard-to-reach places to remove moisture, apply an anti-corrosive layer that never dries out, and slow down any rusting that may already have started. It can be time and money well spent, depending on how long you intend keeping your vehicle.

Inside story

Owners of very elderly Shoguns and Pajeros won't find this section of the chapter particularly useful, as they're unlikely to be too worried about the condition and maintenance of their vehicles' interiors. After all, any hard-working 4x4 that's been around more than 20 years will be 'boasting' a well worn interior by now, with the leather used on imported early Pajeros being particularly prone to wear and rips. For the rest of us, how we treat the insides of our 4x4s can have a significant effect on residuals when the time comes to sell.

I'm not going to insult you by hinting that you empty your ashtray every so often and vacuum your carpets from time to time. If, however, you intend taking your

Rust like this could so easily have been avoided. A build-up of mud and road salt behind the front wing, and a chipping away of paint on the outer surface, have both contributed to this unsightly corrosion. What a shame. *(Author)*

Another example of how a build-up of mud in a hidden place can cause major damage in later life. This badly bubbling Shogun's front wing is basically scrap now, as beneath that rupturing paint lies serious inside-to-out rot. *(Author)*

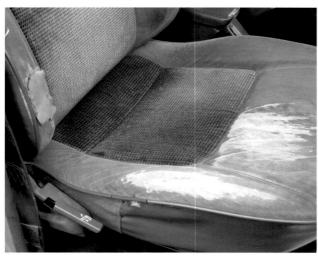

Look after your Mitsubishi's interior and it will stay looking smart for many years to come. When it's gone this bad though, there's very little you can do... *(Author)*

Mitsubishi off-road, I do suggest you spend some money on full-width protective mats for your floor and a set of protective vinyl covers for your seats. You might think it's only the outside of your car that gets muddy when you drive off-road, but it isn't. At some point you'll want to get out of your vehicle, chat with other owners, see what other drivers are getting up to in the mud – and as soon as you climb back inside, you'll be

Mitsubishi's dual-range transfer box and part-time four-wheel drive system are generally very reliable and long lasting. Much, though, depends on how you maintain your vehicle – and how you drive it. *(Author)*

taking all that 'crud' with you. And, make no mistake, ex-quarry mud on your carpets or smeared onto your seats is very difficult indeed to remove properly.

Have a chat with one or two of the 4x4 specialist retailers listed in Appendix A and see what kind of interior protection they have to offer. Spend a few pounds before you head for the mud and, I promise you, it will be a wise investment.

Careful driving

When it comes to looking after any 4x4, one area of concern that many people overlook is that of driving style, particularly when it comes to off-roading. How you drive your Shogun or Pajero can have a major impact on its longevity, reliability and resale value, yet many owners underestimate this vital fact.

Again, I'm not going to stand in judgement and preach about how you should behave when you're behind the wheel. But what I would suggest is that, particularly when it comes to off-road driving, you at least adopt a degree of 'mechanical sympathy'.

Let's take the basic example of Mitsubishi's original dual-range transfer box. Although the principle behind the company's part-time all-wheel-drive set-up has changed relatively little over the years, the transfer box itself has been developed. Later Shoguns and Pajeros feature the 'shift-on-the-fly' set-up mentioned earlier on in the book, which means you don't need to bring your vehicle to a complete standstill in order to select high-ratio four-wheel drive from two-wheel drive. In fact, Mitsubishi claims you can do so at any speed up to 100kmh (62mph). But is this really wise? My argument is, why put extra unnecessary strain on your transfer box and transmission simply to prove a point? Bring your speed down to a more sensible level, then select 4H (or even 4HLc in Series III models) and I'm convinced you'll be doing the whole system a big favour. You're also more likely to be enjoying trouble-free motoring for a long time to come.

An awareness of 'mechanical sympathy' makes for good, effective off-road driving in general. When tackling a steep downward slope, for example, off-road experts recommend you rely on engine braking rather than traditional braking, as this reduces the risk of skidding or going off course. This certainly saves brake wear; and by letting your engine 'do the work' with no acceleration on your part, you're reducing its wear and tear in general. Diesel-engined 4x4s tend to offer superior engine braking to petrol models because of their increased torque lower down the rev range;

however, most Shoguns offer a combination of decent torque and more than adequate engine braking for general tough-terrain situations.

When driving off-road, avoiding any drastic or sudden manoeuvres will help reduce the risk of mechanical damage. It's always tempting to aim for the roughest section of a track, the steepest part of an incline, the deepest area of a lake or the rockiest section of a course, but don't forget you'll be risking both mechanical and bodywork damage as a result, and if you're relying on your 4x4 to get you to work the next morning, it's a point worth remembering.

Towing advice

With a large proportion of Shogun/Pajero owners using their vehicles as tow cars, this is another vital area to consider when planning the maintenance and general care of your Mitsubishi. Much of the safety of your complete car and caravan outfit relies on the general condition of your Shogun or Pajero, so to assume that all is well at all times can be a big mistake.

As mentioned in previous chapters, making sure that your Mitsubishi is big enough, powerful enough and heavy enough for the job in hand is absolutely

Careful off-road driving is another key to any 4x4's reliability. Smooth, steady progress through tough terrain will get you there safely and without excess strain on your Shogun/Pajero. Developing an appreciation of 'mechanical sympathy' helps both the vehicle and your driving experience. *(Author)*

essential. It's equally important that you carry out all the necessary research related to this before you buy either the caravan/trailer or the Mitsubishi.

Did you know, for example (assuming you're into extra-large caravans), that a caravan in excess of 2.3 metres in width or 7.0 metres in length can only be legally towed in the UK by what's classed as a 'heavy motor vehicle' – that is, one with a gross vehicle weight of more than 3500 kilograms? As the National Caravan Council (NCC) says on its website, 'Not even a Transit van, nor the biggest 4x4, can lawfully tow a caravan that exceeds these dimensions.'

Whether you're experienced at towing or a first-timer, it may well be worth getting hold of a copy of the NCC's excellent booklet: *The Caravan Towing Code*. It contains lots of recommendations reviewed and agreed by the Driving Standards Agency and is supported by both The Caravan Club and The Camping &

Caravanning Club. You can obtain your own copy from any NCC dealer member or by emailing the NCC direct at: info@nationalcaravan.co.uk.

What does all this have to do with looking after your Shogun/Pajero? More than you think; after all, by learning more about the kinds of caravans and trailers your vehicle can tow, as well as tips on actually driving with a caravan bringing up the rear, you can do a lot to prevent unnecessary strain on your vehicle and any kind of resultant damage.

The NCC is also able to offer essential information on the best way to load a caravan, the advantages of stabilisers, how breakaway cables work, looking after your caravan's wheels and tyres and a whole lot more. Any such advice that helps you to make your caravan-towing experience safer and more pleasurable will also have a positive effect on your vehicle and its long-term condition. Check out the NCC's website for the full rundown: www.nationalcaravan.co.uk.

Over to you

Whether you're about to start looking for a Shogun or Pajero to buy or you're already the proud owner of one, this book should have given you the information you need when it comes to general ownership and getting the most from your Mitsubishi. Whatever you take from

If you're a first-time caravan owner and would appreciate some expert advice, there's no shortage of organisations willing to help. Getting hold of a copy of *The Caravan Towing Code* is a wise first step. (Author)

the book, though, you can be confident you've chosen one of the finest all-round 4x4s ever to come out of Japan – and that's quite a boast when you bear in mind some of the excellent competition.

You'll no doubt make lots of your own decisions along the way. Do you buy a Shogun or go for an imported Pajero? Do you need a long- or a short-wheelbase version? Are you a diesel fan or a petrolhead? Will you buy your parts from a Mitsubishi dealer or from a Japanese 4x4 specialist? Will you get your insurance from a mainstream provider or a specialist broker? Will you be using your Mitsubishi every day or keeping it specifically for towing the family caravan? These – and many more – questions can and should be asked, and the answers will vary from person to person.

The good news is that the variety of answers available have, by and large, been covered somewhere in this book – and that means a Shogun/Pajero experience that should be exactly right for you.

Enjoy your vehicle. You've made an excellent choice.

Above: Your final choice of Shogun/Pajero specification will depend on several factors – not least your family needs and your available budget. Get the mix right and you'll have a 4x4 more than capable of fulfilling your requirements, no matter which generation you end up owning. *(Mitsubishi)*

Below: It's hard to think of another family-size 4x4 that performs so many essential roles with quite such aplomb. For many enthusiasts, though, it will always be the Series II models that stand out from the crowd. For second-hand value for money combined with reliability and sheer practicality, there's little to touch them. Buy with confidence. *(Mitsubishi)*

Specialists, clubs & contacts

SPECIALISTS
(SPARES & ACCESSORIES)

Diamond Auto Parts

Brookbank Garage, Scotland Road, Carnforth,
Lancashire LA5 9JZ.
Tel: 01524 734200. Website:
www.diamondautoparts.co.uk.
Email: sales@diamondautoparts.co.uk.
*Suppliers of parts and accessories for all
Mitsubishis.*

Mitsubishi Parts Online

Website: www.mitsubishipartsonline.co.uk.
Email: mitsubishiparts@courtandsmith.co.uk.
*Online suppliers of parts and accessories for all Pajeros,
Shoguns and derivatives.*

Milner Off Road

Old Hackney Lane, Matlock,
Derbyshire DE4 2QJ.
Tel: 01629 734411. Fax: 01629 733906.
Website: www.milneroffroad.com.
Email: sales@milneroffroad.com.
*Specialists in parts and accessories for Japanese 4x4s;
established since 1981.*

Auto Japanese Spares

110 Eastcotes, Tile Hill,
Coventry CV4 9AS.
Tel: 02476 474848. Fax: 02476 695700.
Website: www.autojapspares.co.uk.
Email: sales@autojapspares.co.uk.
*Suppliers of parts and accessories for all Shoguns and
Pajeros.*

Specialist Leisure

Unit D2, Taylor Business Park, Risley, Warrington,
Cheshire WA3 6BH.
Tel: 01925 768833. Fax: 01925 768866.
Email: info@specialist-leisure.co.uk
Website: www.specialist-leisure.co.uk
Importers of 4x4 accessories.

Thornton Breakers

755 Thornton Road, Thornton, Bradford, West Yorkshire
BD13 3NW.
Tel: 01274 834790. Fax: 01274 831019.
Website: www.thorntonbreakers.co.uk.
Email: thorntonbreakers@btconnect.com.
*Dismantlers of most 4x4s, including Shoguns, Pajeros
and L200s.*

LA Supertrux

18 Lanchester Way, Royal Oak Industrial Estate,
Daventry, Northamptonshire NN11 5PH.
Tel: 01327 705456. Fax: 01327 871786.
Website: www.supertrux.com
Suppliers of 4x4 accessories and off-road modifications.

Japanese 4x4 Spares

Birmingham Motor Parts, 610A Coventry Road,
Smallheath, Birmingham B10 0US.
Tel/Fax: 0121 766 6008.
Email: sales@japanese4x4spares.co.uk
Website: www.japanese4x4spares.co.uk
*Suppliers of new parts for all Japanese 4x4s, including
Shoguns and Pajeros.*

Road & Trail

Church Road, Leverington, Nr. Wisbech,
Cambridgeshire PE13 5DE.
Tel: 01945 465337. Fax: 01945 476421.
Email: road.trail@talk21.com
Website: www.roadandtrail4x4.co.uk
Specialist 4x4 breakers; Shogun/Pajero parts usually in stock.

Explorer UK

Poplar Park, Cliff Lane, Lymm, Cheshire WA13 0TD.
Tel: 01925 757588.
Fax: 01925 755146.
Email: sales@explorerprocomp.co.uk
Website: www.explorerprocomp.co.uk
Suppliers of suspension kits, replacement springs and damper upgrades.

Formula 4x4

Stafford Road, Stone, Staffordshire ST15 0UN.
Tel: 01785 811211.
Fax: 01785 817788. Email: info@formula4x4.com
Website: www.formula4x4.com
Suppliers of general 4x4 accessories and upgrades.

4x4 Accessories & Tyres

Mercury Park, Leeming Bar Industrial Estate, Leeming
Bar, North Yorkshire DL7 9UN. Tel: 01677 425555.
Fax: 01677 425666.
Email: sales@4x4accessoriesandtyres.com
Website: www.4x4accessoriesandtyres.com
Suppliers of general 4x4 accessories. Wheels and tyres a speciality.

Scorpion Racing 4x4 Centre

Unit D, The Coppetts Centre, North Circular Road,
London N12 0SH.
Tel: 020 8211 4888. Fax: 020 8211 4999.
Website: www.scorpion-racing.co.uk
Suppliers of standard and uprated 4x4 parts and accessories, including suspension and brake upgrades.

GT 4x4

Vange Park Road, Five Bells, Basildon, Essex.
Tel: 01268 584585.
Fax: 01268 550292.
Website: www.gtfourxfour.com.
Email: sales@gtfourxfour.com.
Dismantlers of most 4x4s, including Shoguns and Pajeros.

CLN 4x4

78–80 Church Street, Chalvey, Slough,
Berkshire SL1 2PE. Tel: 01753 570112.
Fax: 01753 570114. Email: info@cln.ltd.uk
Website: www.cln.ltd.uk
Suppliers of 4x4 bull bars, styling accessories and spare wheel covers.

Warn Winches

Arbil Ltd., Providence Street, Lye, Stourbridge, West
Midlands DY9 8HS.
Tel: 01384 895700. Fax: 01384 898645.
Website: www.arbil.co.uk
UK importers of American-built Warn winches and lifting gear.

West Coast Off-Road Centre

Gorsey Lane, Banks, Southport.
Tel: 01704 229014. Fax: 01704 232911.
Suppliers of Ironman 4x4 suspension upgrades.

Bronco 4x4

25 Broad Street, Leek, Staffordshire ST13 5NX.
Tel: 01538 398555.
Fax: 01538 398333. Email: sales@bronco4x4.com
Website: www.bronco4x4.com
Off-road wheel and tyre specialists.

Equicar 4x4

Athena Works, Meadow Lane, Coseley, Nr.
Wolverhampton, West Midlands WV14 9NQ.
Tel: 01902 882883. Fax: 01902 882855.
Email: sales@equicar4x4.co.uk
Website: www.equicar4x4.co.uk
Specialist 4x4 breakers, usually with Shogun/Pajero parts in stock.

Bromleys

Leigh St, Chorley, Lancashire PR7 3DS. Tel: 01257 274100.
Website: www.tunit.co.uk. Email: info@tunit.co.uk.
Manufacturers and retailers of the Tunit range of power upgrades for diesel-engined vehicles.

Van Aaken Developments

Crowthorne Business Centre, Telford Avenue,
Crowthorne, Berkshire RG45 6XA. Tel: 01344 777553.
Fax: 01344 777557. Website: www.vanaaken.com.
Email: vanaaken@vanaaken.com.
Manufacturers and retailers of power upgrade systems for diesel-engined vehicles.

Auto Styling UK

Wednesfield Way Industrial Estate, Well Lane,
Wednesfield, Wolverhampton WV11 1XP.
Tel: 0845 644 4704. Fax: 0845 644 5014.
Email: sales@autostylinguk.com.
Suppliers of 4x4 accessories and upgrades.

Direct 4x4

Tel: 01332 601016. Fax: 01332 743102.
Website: www.direct4x4.co.uk.
Email: sales@direct4x4.co.uk.
Specialists in customised spare wheel covers, plus other Shogun/Pajero accessories.

Design-A-Cover

Unit 1, Victoria Business Centre, Neilston Street,
Leamington Spa CV31 2AZ. Tel: 0870 750 1144.
Website: www.design-a-cover.com.
Specialists in customised spare wheel covers to your own design.

Hardtops Direct

Maurice Gaymer Road, Attleborough, Norfolk N17 2QZ.
Tel: 0800 298 8018.
Website: www.hardtopsdirect.co.uk. Email:
sales@hardtopsdirect.co.uk.
Manufacturers and suppliers of hard-tops for L200 and other pick-ups.

Glassfibre UK

Hangar 5, Long Lane, Throckmorton, Pershore,
Worcesteshire WR10 2JH.
Tel: 01386 555787.
Website: www.glassfibresuk.com.
Email: glassfibres@btconnect.com.
Manufacturers and suppliers of hard-tops for L200 and other pick-ups.

SPECIALISTS
(IMPORTS, SALES, TOWING, ETC.)

BIMTA

British Independent Motor Trade Association, 1st Floor,
14B Chapel Place, Tunbridge Wells, Kent TN1 1YQ.
Tel: 01892 515425. Fax: 01892 515495.
Website: www.bimta.co.uk. Email: queries@bimta.org.
Trade association for the UK's independent vehicle import industry. Suppliers of BIMTA certificates of authentification for imported vehicles.

VOSA

Vehicle and Operator Services Agency, Berkeley House,
Croydon Street, Bristol BS5 ODA.
Tel: 0117 954 3200. Fax: 0117 9543212.
Website: www.vosa.gov.uk.
Email: enquiries@vosa.gov.uk.
Official Government body responsible for ESVA testing and legislation. Check out the website for further details of ESVA system.

Protechnical Ltd.

23 Clevedon Road, Nailsea, Bristol BS48 1EW.
Tel: 01275 859955. Fax: 01275 859944.
Website: www.protech-uk.co.uk.
Email: carsales@protech-uk.co.uk.
Specialists in SVA preparation and conversions; also sales of imported Japanese vehicles.

Stuart Spencer Autos

Dudley Port, Tipton, West Midlands DY4 7RG.
Tel: 0121 557 7795.
Fax: 0121 557 7797.
Website: www.ssautos.co.uk.
Email: ssautos@fsnet.co.uk.
Specialist importers and retailers of used Pajeros, Delicas and other Japanese 4x4s.

Antrac Motors

Rock Garage, Quakers Yard,
Mid Glamorgan.
Tel: 01443 410389. Mobile: 07831 838833.
Specialist importers and retailers of used Pajeros, Delicas and other Japanese 4x4s.

Bristol Import Centre

83–93 Fishponds Road, Bristol BS5 6PN.
Tel: 01179 525955.
Website: www.bristolimportcentre.co.uk.
Email: sales@bristolimportcentre.co.uk.
Specialist importers and retailers of used Pajeros and other Japanese 4x4s.

Allan's Vehicle Services

The Yard, Wixenford Farm, Plymstock,
Plymouth PL9 8AA.
Tel: 01752 700270. Mobile: 07970 301013.
Website: www.allansvehicleservices.co.uk.
Email: allan@allansvehicleservices.co.uk.
Specialist importer and retailer of used Pajeros, Delicas and other Japanese 4x4s.

Worcester Road Motors
Worcester Road, Stourport-on-Severn,
Worcestershire DY13 9AS.
Tel: 01299 822239. Fax: 01299 822239.
Website: www.worcesterroadmotors.co.uk.
Retailers of imported used Pajeros and Delicas.

Exceeds.co.uk
2 Vale Road, Northfleet, Kent DA11 8BZ.
Tel: 01474 535852.
Website: www.exceeds.co.uk.
Email: sales@exceeds.co.uk.
Specialist importer of used Pajeros, particularly Exceed model.

Family Cars From Robert Tart
Hoo Garage, Gloucester Road, Tewkesbury,
Gloucester GL20 7DA.
Tel: 01684 275566. Fax: 01684 275567.
Website: www.familycarsuk.com.
Email: sales@familycarsuk.com.
Importers and retailers of used Pajeros from Japan, plus parts and accessories.

Select 4WD
Tel: 01934 627233. Fax: 01934 413700.
Website: www.select4wd.com.
Email: sales@select4wd.com.
Retail suppliers of new Japanese pick-ups, including Mitsubishi L200.

Far East Services
PO Box 5, Bexley, Kent DA5 2ZZ. Tel: 01322 865400.
Fax: 01322 865402.
Website: www.importedvehicles.co.uk.
Email: manager@importedvehicles.co.uk.
Specialists in imports of all makes/models of used Japanese vehicles.

Batfa Japan Inc.
Setagaya-ku, Tokyo 154-0017, Japan.
Tel: 81 3 3413 8080.
Email: info@batfa.com
Exporters of new and used vehicles from Japan to almost any location.

Towsafe
Website: www.towsafe.co.uk. Email: towsafe@hpi.co.uk.
HPI's car-and-caravan-matching database, offering easy access to official statistics and towing capacities.

National Caravan Council
Catherine House, Victoria Road, Aldershot,
Hampshire GU11 1SS.
Tel:01252 318251.
Fax: 01252 322596. Website:
www.nationalcaravan.co.uk.
Email: info@nationalcaravan.co.uk.
National body of the caravan industry, also offering invaluable advice for both experienced and first-time caravanners.

AUCTION HOUSES ('GREY' IMPORTS)

Motor Way Car Auctions
Tel: 02380 710022

Global Vehicle Imports
Tel: 02380 710022

A1 Car Auctions
02380 839009

Overseas International Cars (Wholesalers)
02380 384350

Japanese Motor Auctions
0151 922 5333

Durham County Motor Auctions
01740 650065

Car Auctions UK
01332 850309

OFFICIAL ESVA TESTING STATIONS

Aberdeen
Cloverhill Road, Bridge of Don Industrial Estate,
Aberdeen AB23 8FE.
Tel: 01224 702357.

Beverley
Oldbeck Road, Off Grovehill Road, Beverley HU17 0JG.
Tel: 01482 881522.

Birmingham
Garretts Green Industrial Estate, Birmingham B33 0SS.
Tel: 0121 783 6560.

Bristol
Unit 10, IO Centre, Moreend Avenue, Poplar Way West,
Avonmouth, Bristol BS11 0QL. Tel: 0117 938 1157.

Cardiff (Llantrisant)
School Road, Miskin, Pontyclun, Mid Glamorgan
CF72 8YR. Tel: 01443 224701.

Carlisle
Brunthill Road, Kingstown Industrial Estate, Carlisle
CA3 0EH. Tel: 01228 528106.

North Manchester (Chadderton)
Broadway Business Park, Broadgate, Chadderton,
Oldham OL9 9XA.
Tel: 0161 947 1000.

Chelmsford
Widford Industrial Estate, Chelmsford, Essex CM1 3AE.
Tel: 01245 259341.

Derby
Curzon Lane, Alverston, Derby DE21 7HT.
Tel: 01332 571961.

Exeter
Grace Road, Marsh Barton Trading Estate, Exeter
EX2 8PH. Tel: 01392 217276.

Gillingham
Ambley Road, Gillingham, Kent ME8 0SJ.
Tel: 01634 232541.

Glasgow (Bishopbriggs)
Crosshill Road, Bishopbriggs, Glasgow G64 2QA.
Tel: 0141 7726321.

Leighton Buzzard
Stanbridge Road, Leighton Buzzard LU7 8QG.
Tel: 01525 373074.

Liverpool (Speke)
South Liverpool Commercials, Woodend Avenue, Speke,
Liverpool L24 9NB.
Tel: 0151 486 0050 / 0151 547 4445.

West London (Yeading)
Cygnet Way, Willow Tree Lane, Yeading, Hayes,
Middlesex UB4 9BS.
Tel: 0208 841 9205.

North London (Edmonton)
Towpath Road (off Harbet Road), Lea Valley Trading
Estate, Edmonton, London N18 3JR. Tel: 0208 803 7733.

South London (Mitcham)
Redhouse Road, Croydon, Surrey CR0 3AQ. Tel: 0208
684 1499.

Newcastle-upon-Tyne
Sandy Lane, Gosforth, Newcastle-upon-Tyne NE3 5HB.
Tel: 0191 236 5011.

Norwich
Jupiter Road, Hellesden, Norwich NR6 6SS. Tel: 01603
408128.

Nottingham
Main Road, Watnall, Nottingham NH6 1JF. Tel: 0115 938
2591.

Shrewsbury
SVA Site, Levens Drive, Harlescott, Shrewsbury SY1
3EG. Tel: 01743 462621.

Southampton
Unit R, Centurion Industrial Estate, Bitterne Road West,
Southampton SO18 1UB. Tel: 02380 837397.

Taunton
Taunton Trading Estate, Norton Fitzwarren, Taunton,
Somerset TA2 6RX.
Tel: 01823 282525.

CLUBS

The Mitsubishi Pajero & Shogun Owners' Club
Club Secretary: Ray Waller, 22 Nightingale Lane, Feltwell,
Thetford, Norfolk IP26 4AR.
Website: www.psoc.org.uk.
Email: membership@psoc.org.uk.
*Founded in 1999, this UK-based club boasts almost
2000 members and offers a regular magazine, technical
advice, social events and a members' website.*

Pajero Owners' Club UK
Website: www.pocuk.com. Email: admin@pocuk.com.
*Founded in 2001, this Internet-based club offers free
membership and numerous benefits including negotiated
discounts with parts suppliers and specialists.*

Mitsubishi Owners' Club

Watermoor, Cirencester, Gloucestershire GL7 1LF.
Website: www.mitsubishi-cars.co.uk.
Email ownerc@mitsubishi-cars.co.uk.
Official club for all Mitsubishi vehicles, launched and run
by the company's British operations.

Mitsubishi L200 Owners' Club

Website: www.L200.org.uk.
Email: contact@L200.org.uk.
British club catering for commercial and non-commercial
owners of all L200 pick-ups.

Mitsubishi Owners' Club (Netherlands)

Aletta Jacobshof 8, 7908 BX Hoogeveen, The Netherlands.
Website: www.mitsubishi-owners-club.nl. Email:
info@mitsubishi-owners-club.nl.
Active club catering for owners of all Mitsubishis in The
Netherlands and Europe.

Mitsubishi Four Wheel Drive Club of America

Contact: Ray Sala, Club Secretary.
Tel: (001) 408-346-1421.
Website:
www.geocities.com/mitsubishifourwheeldriveclub.
Email: mitsubishifourwheeldriveclub@yahoo.com.
American-based club welcoming owners of all
Mitsubishi 4x4s.

Mitsubishi 4WD Owners' Club of Queensland

PO Box 1055, Milton, Brisbane, Queensland 4064, Australia.
Website: www.mitsu4wdclubqld.org.
Email: membership@mitsu4wdclubqld.org.
Australian club catering for owners of all four-wheel-drive
Mitsubishis.

The All Wheel Drive Club

PO Box 186, Uckfield TN22 3YQ. Tel: 01825 731875.
Website: www.awdc.co.uk
Founded in 1968, the AWDC welcomes all 4x4 owners
and organises various off-road events. Free bi-monthly
magazine for members.

The Caravan Club

East Grinstead House, East Grinstead, West Sussex
RH19 1UA. Tel: 01342 326944. Fax: 01342 410258.
Website: www.caravanclub.co.uk.
Email: enquiries@caravanclub.co.uk.
Large club for all UK-based caravanners offering many
benefits, including access to exclusive club caravan sites.

The Camping & Caravanning Club

Greenfields House, Westwood Way, Coventry CV4 8JH.
Tel: 02476 694995.
Website: www.campingandcaravanningclub.co.uk.
Large club representing the interests of British camping
and caravanning enthusiasts.

The Green Lane Association

PO Box 48, Huntingdon, Cambridgeshire PE26 2YY.
Email: membership@glass-uk.org
Website: www.glass-uk.org
Organisation dedicated to preserving vehicular rights of
way and promoting sensible driving in the countryside.

OFF-ROAD SITES & ORGANISERS

4x4 Funday

The Beeches, Llanidloes, Powys SY18 6EP.
Tel: 01686 413151. Fax: 01686 413040.
Email: richard@4x4funday.co.uk
Website: www.4x4funday.co.uk
Organisers of non-competitive off-road fun days in
Warwickshire, Worcestershire, Shropshire and
Lancashire. Typical costs start at £30 per vehicle per day.

Motor Safari

Unit 230B, Redwither Central, Redwither Business Park,
Wrexham LL13 9UE.
Tel: 01978 754533. Fax: 01978 754534.
Email: info@motor-safari.co.uk
Website: www.motor-safari.co.uk
Off-road adventure driving and green laning at venues
throughout the UK.

Trailmasters International

Tel: 01691 649194.
Email: info@trailmasters.com
Website: www.trailmasters.com
Organisers of overseas off-road safaris and UK-based
4x4 weekends.

Langdale Quest

Bickley Rigg Farm, Bickley, Langdale End, Scarborough,
North Yorkshire YO13 0LL.
Tel: 01723 882335. Fax: 01723 882375.
Email: info@langdalequest.co.uk
Website: www.langdalequest.co.uk
10,000-acre off-road centre, claimed to be the largest of
its kind in the UK.

Yorkshire 4x4

Tel: 0800 298 6488. Website: www.yorkshire4x4.co.uk.
Email: info@yorkshire4x4.co.uk.
Purpose-built off-road courses situated throughout Yorkshire.

Sahara Travel

Abbey House, Dublin 1, Ireland. Tel: 00353 1 496 8844.
Website: www.saharatravel.com.
Specialists in off-road exploration holidays to Northern Africa – Algeria, Libya and Tunisia.

GLOBAL MITSUBISHI

Official websites:
Austria – www.mitsubishi-motors.at
Belgium – www.mitsubishi-motors.be
Bulgaria – www.mitsubishi-motors.bg
Croatia – www.mitsubishi-motors.com.hr
Cyprus – www.fairways.com.cy
Czech Republic – www.mitsubishi.cz
Denmark – www.mitsubishi.dk
Estonia – www.mitsubishi-motors.ee

Finland – www.mitsubishi.fi
France – www.mitsubishi-motors.fr
Germany – www.mitsubishi-motors.de
Greece – www.mitsubishi-motors.gr
Hungary – www.mitsubishimotors.co.hu
Iceland – www.mitsubishi-motors.is
Ireland – www.mitsubishi-motors.ie
Israel – www.mitsubishi-israel.co.il
Italy – www.mitsubishi-auto.it
Japan – www.mitsubishi.com
Luxembourg – www.mitsubishi-motors.lu
The Netherlands – www.mitsubishi-motors.nl
Norway – www.mitsubishi-motors.no
Poland – www.mitsubishi.com.pl
Portugal – www.mitsubishi.pt
Romania – www.mitsubishiromania.ro
Russia – www.mitsubishi-motors.ru/ru
Spain – www.mitsubishi-motors-europe.com
Sweden – www.mitsubishi.nu
Switzerland – www.mitsubishi.ch
Turkey – www.temsa.com.tr
Ukraine – www.mitsubishi-ukraine.com.ua
United Kingdom – www.mitsubishi-cars.co.uk
USA – www.mitsubishicars.com

Appendix B

Technical specifications

SHOGUN/PAJERO SERIES I (2600)

ENGINE:	2555cc four-cylinder in-line petrol
MAX POWER:	102bhp @ 4500rpm
MAX TORQUE:	142lb ft @ 2500rpm
PERFORMANCE:	Max speed 88mph, 0–60mph 14.5 secs
ECONOMY:	17.1mpg (urban); 25.9mpg (at 56mph); 17.5mpg (at 75mph)
TRANSMISSION:	Five-speed manual
DRIVE:	Part-time four-wheel drive; dual-range transfer box
STEERING:	Power-assisted recirculating ball and nut
BRAKES:	Front discs; rear drums
SUSPENSION:	Independent front suspension with twin wishbones; rear leaf springs
OVERALL LENGTH:	181ins (five-door); 155ins (three-door)
OVERALL WIDTH:	66.1ins
OVERALL HEIGHT:	74ins (low-roof); 76.6ins (high-roof)

SHOGUN/PAJERO SERIES I (2.3 TD)

ENGINE:	2346cc four-cylinder in-line turbo diesel
MAX POWER:	84bhp @ 4200rpm
MAX TORQUE:	132lb ft @ 2000rpm
PERFORMANCE:	Max speed 82mph, 0–60mph 19.0 secs
ECONOMY:	N/A
TRANSMISSION:	Five-speed manual
DRIVE:	Part-time four-wheel drive; dual-range transfer box
STEERING:	Power-assisted recirculating ball and nut
BRAKES:	Front discs; rear drums
SUSPENSION:	Independent front suspension with twin wishbones; rear leaf springs
OVERALL LENGTH:	155ins (three-door)
OVERALL WIDTH:	66.1ins
OVERALL HEIGHT:	74ins

SHOGUN/PAJERO SERIES I (2.5 TD)

ENGINE:	2477cc four-cylinder in-line turbo diesel
MAX POWER:	84bhp @ 4200rpm
MAX TORQUE:	148lb ft @ 2000rpm
PERFORMANCE:	Max speed 83mph, 0–60mph 17.8 secs
ECONOMY:	27mpg (urban); 31mpg (at 56mph); 20mpg (at 75mph)
TRANSMISSION:	Five-speed manual (optional four-speed automatic)
DRIVE:	Part-time four-wheel drive; dual-range transfer box
STEERING:	Power-assisted recirculating ball and nut
BRAKES:	Front discs; rear drums
SUSPENSION:	Independent front suspension with twin wishbones; rear leaf springs
OVERALL LENGTH:	181ins (five-door); 155ins (three-door)
OVERALL WIDTH:	66.1ins
OVERALL HEIGHT:	74ins (low roof); 76.6ins (high roof)

SHOGUN/PAJERO SERIES I (3.0 V6)

ENGINE:	2972cc V6 petrol
MAX POWER:	141bhp
MAX TORQUE:	166lb ft
PERFORMANCE:	Max speed 101mph, 0–60mph 13.6 secs
ECONOMY:	Average 16–20mpg overall
TRANSMISSION:	Five-speed manual (optional four-speed automatic)
DRIVE:	Part-time four-wheel drive; dual-range transfer box
STEERING:	Power-assisted recirculating ball and nut
BRAKES:	Front discs; rear drums
SUSPENSION:	Independent front suspension with twin wishbones; rear leaf springs
OVERALL LENGTH:	181ins (five-door only)
OVERALL WIDTH:	66.1ins
OVERALL HEIGHT:	74ins

SHOGUN/PAJERO SERIES II (2.5 TD)

ENGINE:	2477cc four-cylinder in-line turbo diesel with intercooler
MAX POWER:	105bhp @ 4200rpm
MAX TORQUE:	177lb ft @ 2000rpm
PERFORMANCE:	Max speed 91mph, 0–60mph 17.0 secs
ECONOMY:	Average 25–28mpg overall
TRANSMISSION:	Five-speed manual
DRIVE:	Part-time four-wheel drive; dual-range transfer box; 'shift-on-the-fly' selection
STEERING:	Power-assisted recirculating ball and nut
BRAKES:	Front and rear discs (optional ABS)
SUSPENSION:	Independent front suspension; coil springs all round
OVERALL LENGTH:	186ins (five-door); 163ins (three-door)
OVERALL WIDTH:	67.7ins
OVERALL HEIGHT:	75ins

SHOGUN/PAJERO SERIES II (2.8 TD)

ENGINE:	2835cc four-cylinder in-line turbo diesel with intercooler
MAX POWER:	123bhp @ 4000rpm
MAX TORQUE:	215lb ft @ 2000rpm
PERFORMANCE:	Max speed 94mph, 0–60mph 15.8 secs
ECONOMY:	Average 16–20mpg overall
TRANSMISSION:	Five-speed manual (optional four-speed automatic)
DRIVE:	Part-time four-wheel drive; dual-range transfer box; 'shift-on-the-fly' selection
STEERING:	Power-assisted recirculating ball and nut
BRAKES:	Front and rear discs (optional ABS)
SUSPENSION:	Independent front suspension; coil springs all round
OVERALL LENGTH:	186ins (five-door only)
OVERALL WIDTH:	67.7ins
OVERALL HEIGHT:	75ins

SHOGUN/PAJERO SERIES II (3.0 V6)

ENGINE:	2972cc V6 petrol
MAX POWER:	147bhp @ 5000rpm
MAX TORQUE:	N/A
PERFORMANCE:	Max speed 102mph, 0–60mph 13.2 secs
ECONOMY:	Average 25–28mpg
TRANSMISSION:	Five-speed manual (optional four-speed automatic)
DRIVE:	Part-time four-wheel drive; dual-range transfer box; 'shift-on-the-fly' selection
STEERING:	Power-assisted recirculating ball and nut
BRAKES:	Front and rear discs (optional ABS)
SUSPENSION:	Independent front suspension; coil springs all round
OVERALL LENGTH:	186ins (five-door); 163ins (three-door)
OVERALL WIDTH:	67.7ins
OVERALL HEIGHT:	75ins

SHOGUN/PAJERO SERIES II (3.5 V6)

ENGINE:	3497cc V6 petrol
MAX POWER:	205bhp @ 5000rpm
MAX TORQUE:	221lb ft @ 3000rpm
PERFORMANCE (FIVE-DOOR):	Max speed 107mph, 0–60mph 10.7 secs
PERFORMANCE (THREE-DOOR):	Max speed 116mph, 0–60mph 9.5 secs
ECONOMY:	Average 15–19mpg overall
TRANSMISSION:	Five-speed manual (optional four-speed automatic)
DRIVE:	Part-time four-wheel drive; dual-range transfer box; 'shift-on-the-fly' selection
STEERING:	Power-assisted recirculating ball and nut
BRAKES:	Front and rear discs (optional ABS)
SUSPENSION:	Independent front suspension; coil springs all round
OVERALL LENGTH:	186ins (five-door); 163ins (three-door)
OVERALL WIDTH:	67.7ins
OVERALL HEIGHT:	75ins

SHOGUN/PAJERO SERIES III (3.2 DI-D)

ENGINE:	3200cc direct-injection turbo diesel with intercooler
MAX POWER:	162bhp @ 3800rpm
MAX TORQUE:	275lb ft @ 2000rpm
PERFORMANCE:	Max speed 99mph, 0–60mph 12.8 secs
ECONOMY:	23.2mpg (urban); 35.8mpg (extra urban); 29.7mpg (combined)
TRANSMISSION:	Five-speed manual (optional four-speed automatic)
DRIVE:	Part-time four-wheel drive; dual-range transfer box; 'shift-on-the-fly' selection
STEERING:	Power-assisted rack and pinion
BRAKES:	Front and rear discs; ABS; Electronic Brake-force Distribution
SUSPENSION:	Independent coil-sprung all round with telescopic dampers
OVERALL LENGTH:	4830mm (five-door); 4315mm (three-door)
OVERALL WIDTH:	1885mm
OVERALL HEIGHT:	1885mm (five-door); 1875mm (three-door)

SHOGUN/PAJERO SERIES III (3.5 GDI V6)

ENGINE:	3497cc direct-injection 24-valve DOHC petrol
MAX POWER:	200bhp @ 5000rpm
MAX TORQUE:	235lb ft @ 4000rpm
PERFORMANCE:	Max speed 106mph, 0–60mph 11.8 secs
ECONOMY:	14.2mpg (urban); 25.4mpg (extra urban); 19.9mpg (combined)
TRANSMISSION:	Four-speed automatic
DRIVE:	Part-time four-wheel drive; dual-range transfer box; 'shift-on-the-fly' selection
STEERING:	Power-assisted rack and pinion
BRAKES:	Front and rear discs; ABS; Electronic Brake-force Distribution
SUSPENSION:	Independent coil-sprung all round with telescopic dampers
OVERALL LENGTH:	4830mm (five-door); 4315mm (three-door)
OVERALL WIDTH:	1885mm
OVERALL HEIGHT:	1885mm (five-door); 1875mm (three-door)

Index